Ordinary Saints

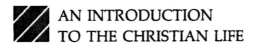

AN INTRODUCTION
TO THE CHRISTIAN LIFE

Ordinary Saints

ROBERT BENNE

Wipf and Stock Publishers
EUGENE, OREGON

For my wife, Joanna,
the most important ordinary saint in my life

And for our children
Kristin, Philip, Michael, Nicholas

The material on p. 172 is from Dag Hammarskjöld, *Markings,* translated by Leif Sjoberg and W. H. Auden, copyright 1964, reprinted by permission of Alfred A. Knopf, Inc.

Wipf and Stock Publishers
199 West 8th Avenue, Suite 3
Eugene, Oregon 97401

Ordinary Saints
An Introduction to the Christian Life
By Benne, Robert
©1988 Augsburg Fortress
ISBN: 1-57910-845-8
Publication date: December, 2001
Previously published by Augsburg Fortress, 1988.

Contents

Preface

Teaching religion and ethics to college students, like facing a firing squad, concentrates the mind wonderfully. It has focused mine on the need—often articulated by those students—for a straightforward and comprehensive account of the Christian life. Throughout an earlier stint of seminary teaching I felt I could safely assume a basic knowledge of Christian moral teaching among those seminarians, and then deal with more refined issues. Toward the latter part of that seventeen-year engagement, I began to sense that even among seminarians knowledge of and agreement with Christian moral teaching was eroding.

Embarking on college teaching has accentuated that intuition. Confusion and uncertainty, as well as curiosity, about religious and moral matters abound among the daughters and sons of mainstream Protestant and Catholic families. They want and need to know what the substance of Christian faith and life is all about.

What seems important in such a context is not extended attention to the issues dealt with in many texts on Christian ethics—inquiries into the method, scope, and sources of Christian ethics. Nor does it seem appropriate to aim primarily at critical reflection on the inherited tradition, as if that tradition were solidly in place. Both approaches, though very important in other contexts, seem to put the cart before the horse in mine.

Instead, I have concentrated on basic instruction in the Christian life, including both its religious and moral dimensions. Having such an aim, I have tried to be clear, comprehensive, and confident. Further, I am commending that Christian life to ordinary people, not to heroes or virtuosi. That is consistent with the Lutheran view of Christian calling which informs this book. Those ordinary people become ordinary saints, not because of either their heroic or ordinary deeds, but because of the extraordinary grace of God in Christ that is freely offered to them. As they receive that grace in faith, they are at the same time called to live Christian lives of faith, love, and hope within the places of responsibility they have been given. This book is simply my effort at sketching out the content and shape of such a life.

This book is characterized by what H. Richard Niebuhr called a "confessional" approach. By that he meant an effort on the part of time- and spacebound persons to state in simple form "what has happened to us in our community, how we came to believe, how we reason about things and what we see from our point of view" (*The Meaning of Revelation* [New York: Macmillan Co., 1960], 29). As such a "confession" this book emphasizes *what* I see from my point of view rather than a defense or justification for what I see. While it is a personal account from a particular point of view, I certainly intend it as more than mere personal opinion. While this book is not strewn with biblical quotations, I hope the Bible speaks through it. I hope the Lutheran tradition permeates its outlook. But, above all, in an age when Christian conviction needs to be clearly expressed, I hope that happens.

I am grateful to Roanoke College for sabbatical leave and to St. Edmund's College of Cambridge University for the hospitable context in which to work. I am indebted to the Siebert Foundation and the Aid Association for Lutherans for financial support, to President Norman Fintel and Vice-President William Miller of Roanoke College for helping me gain that support, and to Carla Barnes for her work on the index. Finally, I am grateful to my wife, Joanna, who not only is the greatest sustainer of my being among all earthly sources, but who also carefully read the text, assessing it for the kind of intelligibility to lay persons that I desire.

Cambridge, England   Robert Benne
June 1986

1

Introduction

LOST IN SPACE

While our society becomes more certain and knowledgeable about technological matters, clarity on our religious, intellectual, and moral moorings wanes ominously. We seem to be developing a huge, muscular body, but one without a central nervous system. We seem uncertain about our purposes, the ends to which all our technological capacities might be applied. This confusion at the social level is both a cause and an effect of confusion at the personal level. It is particularly descriptive of the life of the young, as exposure to life on American college campuses will attest. It is not that virtue is not present. There are many young people with noble inclinations. It is just that those inclinations are not shored up by a firm and confident moral consensus among peers or among the adult members of the community. They are challenged by all sorts of alternative notions of intellectual, moral, and religious ends, some of them not so noble. An uneasy sense of chaos pervades our campuses, a reflection of a broader cultural confusion.

Suicidal gestures and attempts increase even as the external conditions of life improve. Interest in religion is strong while chapel attendance is distressingly low, even considering the traditional rebellion among college students against the forced attendance during their years at home. Students exhibit interest in arcane religious practices but know little of their own heritage. The religious beliefs of historic communities are relegated to the level of opinion, no more compelling than those of the latest rock star. Many of the young wonder why they are at college, let alone why they are on this earth.

Studies are too often linked to crassly utilitarian purposes. At the lowest level are those who study merely to pass in order to satisfy parents who have sent them to college. Courses are merely irritating hurdles placed in their way by devious faculty. At a higher level are those who view their college educations as the necessary accreditation for enhanced life chances. They pass their courses in order to get better jobs. A few pursue their studies toward the intrinsic end of becoming educated persons. These intellectual confusions are too often exacerbated by faculties who themselves cannot agree on the practices becoming a decent education. Schools lose sight of an integrated vision of education as their departments press their own narrow interests.

Moral fragmentation accompanies the religious and intellectual confusion. Symptoms of fragmentation abound. It is difficult to discern effective common grounds to justify limits on the excessive drinking that harms so many young lives, both directly and indirectly. Honors systems that used to regulate student academic behavior have collapsed in most colleges and universities; students and faculty are no longer able to agree on what it means to be honest, let alone what it means to take responsibility for the academic community's integrity. Sexual ethics are essentially relegated to the status of individual opinion and taste. Few are sure whether premarital sex—with its institutionalized variant, cohabitation—is presumed to be right or wrong. It depends upon the circumstances. The double standard erodes but date rape and unwanted sexual encounters amid drunken stupor increase. The true incidence of abortion rarely arises from its darkness to public light. Above all, there is confusion about the moral purposes of education. Are we educated in order to become more productive and conscientious citizens? Are there moral ends that summon the use of our educated talents and energies for the needs of our neighbors? Or, are education and training mostly means to the end of our personal satisfaction and success? Is it best simply to hunker down and pursue that which is marketable at the moment?

Many philosophers and social commentators have analyzed this morass. Among the more well known of these analyses is Alasdair MacIntyre's *After Virtue.* He likens our moral landscape to a hypothetical situation in which a great catastrophe has destroyed most scientific equipment, records, laboratories, and libraries. All that is left are scattered pieces. People use the fragments of scientific knowledge, but the coherent basis of the whole enterprise is destroyed. Another analysis, that of Daniel Bell in his *Cultural Contradictions of Capitalism,* maintains that the motivational system of modern society itself has been undercut by the very success of capitalism. The Protestant ethic, which once motivated and guided our society, has been replaced by the demands of chaotic desire.

While we might argue about the *extent* to which their analyses are true, it is not so debatable that they have pointed to the presence of powerful trends in our society. The religious, intellectual, and moral coherence of our society has eroded. The confusion of our young is one symptom among many. The loss of confidence of the adult world in their own religious, intellectual, and moral convictions is certainly another.

This "lostness" is not simply the product of individual cussedness or recent social upheaval, though both of those factors certainly account for some of it. The problem is much more vast than the frailty of contemporary individuals or society. The confusion is the result of immense historical changes that have had a double-edged effect; much bad has come with these changes alongside the good. At the same time that human knowledge and material achievement have increased dramatically, human religious and moral clarity have waned. This is not to say that there have not been important moral, political, and religious advances during these centuries of historical change, but it is to say that the religious and moral "capital" that generated them has increasingly been depleted. So we seem to be involved in something of a paradox. The great edifice of Western society and culture is resting on a foundation that is shaking.

What has brought this paradox about? We can point to five "triumphs" that have shaped Western societies since the Enlightenment: the triumph of (1) technical reason, (2) historical reason, (3) the liberal spirit, (4) the ethic of self-enhancement, and (5) secularization. Though each is related to and overlaps the other, they can provide categories which help to capture basic trends.

1. By technical reason I mean human transcendence over nature. Human reason is able to grasp the causal connections of natural phenomena. This gives humankind an understanding of the basic workings of nature, and with increased understanding comes the capacity for increased control. This application of technical reason creates technologies that are able to manipulate the basic potencies of nature. The upshot of this application of technical reason to the world has been the magnification and intensification of human powers. The power of human legs to run at twenty miles per hour is extended through technology to travel at five hundred miles per hour in a jet plane. The capacities of the hands to construct crude shelter progress through technology to the construction of one-hundred-story skyscrapers. The ability to eke out a living from the soil with simple tools is transformed by technology to vast mechanized farms. The technical intelligence to fabricate simple products is extended to the construction of huge factories that make the most intricate of products. Human powers are also intensified. The power of the eye to see small things is intensified by technology to see and control elements and processes too small for the unaided human eye.

One could multiply examples of such an extension of human power through the application of technical reason. The result of all this is wondrous. We have been able to wrest from nature a level of living that far transcends the pressures of survival. The wealth produced by the triumph of technical reason has enabled us to live in relative security and comfort. It has enabled many of us to pursue ends that earlier were limited to the privileged few. We can travel and communicate in a rapid manner. We can pursue higher education. While there are still some among us in Western societies who do not participate fully in these achievements of technology, the benefits are widely dispersed.

There is no doubt that the triumph of technical reason has brought magnificent benefits. But there are ambiguities. Technological change quickens social change. It increases mobility. It overturns our parochial identities. It changes our inherited tightly knit communities into patterns of association in which we choose our companions and living space. It shatters old means of production and the way of life that went with them. The magnification of human powers means that we can more easily destroy ourselves and our natural environment.

The affluence generated by technical capacities tempts us to reject necessary restraints and pursue our limitless desires.

In short, one of the effects of technological change, along with its benefits, is the confusion we talked about earlier. Accelerating and pervasive social changes *are* confusing. The expansion of our horizons can be confusing as well as enlightening. Affluence brings disorientation as well as comfort. It is no accident that the most technically advanced societies are also the ones most worried about their spiritual and moral foundations. A fascinating illustration of this worry concerns the ethical issue of abortion, as well as other issues at the border of life and death. Technical capacities have made abortion a relatively easy and safe technique, at least physically speaking. On the other hand, medical advances have enabled us to know much more about the complex life of the fetus at a very early stage, and have increased the capacity to sustain babies outside the womb at ever-earlier points in their development. These technical advances raise issues that we did not have to face before, but the issues are raised in an environment where there is little consensus at the religious and moral level. These issues, difficult enough in their own right, are made more perplexing in a society that has little clarity at the level of meaning and value.

2. Another element in our confused state is the triumph of historical reason. If technical reason gives humans transcending power over natural processes, historical reason, in a curious turn of the table, demonstrates our radical immersion in time and space. The rise of historical reason is of course connected to the rise of technical reason. More rapid transportation and communication, as well as the increased affluence that enabled societies to sustain them, resulted in investigation of societies distant from us in both time and space. Western humans became conscious of their own cultural relativity. We have become conscious that in the long and large sweep of things our view of reality is one among many. Further, natural sciences have shown us that human historical life is a mere blip in the history of our earth, and our earth is a mere speck in a vast universe.

In short, our seemingly secure and privileged place in the world has been overturned. Moreover, we have no certain way to transcend our relativity in time and space. Time and history are in us, even as we are in time and history. This modern consciousness makes simple claims to absolute truth and morality difficult at best. There is no direct access to transhistorical truth. Even though we might make claims for a revealed religious and moral truth, which in fact I will do later, it is also clear that those claims are made from within time- and spacebound communities. There is no clear universal viewpoint outside history from which we can unerringly adjudicate between claims of truth and moral rightness. Although the human effort to find that viewpoint is noble and necessary, it is obvious that the claims made for a universal, rationally based morality sound ever so much like the Western morality shaped decisively by Judeo-Christian history. The moral principles proposed by philosophers as the products of human reason often appear to be rational explications of the Golden Rule.

If these effects of historical reason do not make claims for religious and moral absoluteness seem shaky, further applications of historical reason in their Freudian and Marxist guises will. Both Sigmund Freud and Karl Marx were nineteenth-century masters of discerning hidden agenda. Freud pointed to the hidden presence of unconscious sexual factors in our religious, social, and moral practices. Marx discerned the economic interests of the dominant classes that secretly reigned in those practices. Both were "masters of the hermeneutic of suspicion." Both unmasked the compelling, but hidden, interests in the human practices. Things are never as they seem. Thus, contemporary liberation theologies of various types call into question the inherited religious and moral "truths" of all traditions. These "truths" are distorted by the hidden agenda of those who shaped them. The difficult problem then ensues: how does one sift out the persisting values of a tradition from the distorted notions of the hidden agenda? One upshot of this whole project, as one might expect, is confusion. What can be trusted as sources of sure guidance? Too often among the liberationists the search for guidance results in the adoption of some neo-Marxist framework which substitutes for the "establishment's" inherited tradition. Then, naturally, in a fair turnabout, the hermeneutic of suspicion can be applied to that framework.

Thus confusion multiplies. Can religious and moral beliefs be deemed anything more than personal preference? Can they be more than reflections of the interests of oppressors? Is there any ground upon which to make claim for truth? Such questions point to the quandary posed by historical reason.

3. A third element in our current confusion has been the triumph of the liberal spirit since the Enlightenment of the eighteenth century. The dominant mark of the Enlightenment was its confidence in the capacity of unencumbered Reason to ascertain the good, the true, and the beautiful. After the heavy hand of dark superstition and authority was thrown off the human project, Reason would be able to reach true conclusions in science, politics, art, religion, morality, economics, and education. Rational harmony was the underlying principle of the order of the universe and humankind as rational beings had access to that principle. Thus, as human actions became more rational and more free from the control of authority and tradition, a more harmonious existence would emerge. Coercion would diminish and rational persuasion triumph in human affairs. Out of this spirit came powerful contributions to the development of natural science, political democracy, market economic systems, liberal education, autonomous morality, and liberal religion. Toleration and reasonableness were intended to permeate all those developments, and in fact, did, to a degree. The liberal spirit has made enduring contributions to Western achievements, and we would be considerably poorer without it.

The movement of the liberal spirit in history has not been unambiguous, however. First, it had the tendency to disparage particular historical communities and their traditions. The organic continuities of communal life were often regarded as vestiges of superstition. It was only the promptings of Reason that could be trusted. Less and less regard was relegated to historical communities of faith and local culture, particularly by the intellectual elite who were most likely to bear the liberal spirit. In ethics, for example, the effort of the liberal spirit was to detach the foundations of morality from the practices of historical communities and to ground them in universal Reason. Thus, the "enlightened" members of society were weaned away from attachments to the communities that shaped their lives. Moreover, the relativizing impact of historical and critical reason further sapped the confidence of the educated in those traditions. Education in our elite Western universities often exhibits such characteristics.

Second, the very estimate of Reason has been changed. History has cut Reason down to size, from the glory of Reason, with its capacities to discern goodness, truth, and beauty, to reason, with its capacities to think consistently and clearly. Reason as substantive guidance has given way to reason as instrumentality. Thus, reason searches out the means to reach our desires. Even so, we maintain a respect for the free rationality of the agent so that the free consent of the agent continues as a hallmark of Western morality. In the area of ethics, then, the legislating capacity of reason becomes thinner and thinner. Moral life consists of whatever consenting adults will agree to. Thus, the "triumph of the liberal spirit" is somewhat misleading. The liberal spirit was healthy and positive as long as it had the substance of Western Judeo-Christian civilization to criticize, alter, reform, and "enlighten." It was not really Reason that was guiding things, but rather it was the deposit of those faith communities, enriched by classical traditions, that was being revised by the critical and liberal capacities of humankind to be a fit instrument for Western intentionality. As that deposit was increasingly qualified by the spirit of the Enlightenment, relativized by historical reason, and made increasingly problematic by scientific and technical reason, the liberal spirit itself has become markedly impoverished. Without the substance of tradition to reform, it becomes increasingly empty and impotent to guide either personal or public life. Therefore, our politics become the clash of interest groups rather than the subject of rational debate. Liberal education loses its coherent base and degenerates into the competition of disciplines. Liberal economics abstracts "economic man" from the restraints of culture and society, assuming untrammeled self-interest as the spring of motivation. Liberal religion becomes a congeries of debating societies devoted to further liberation from tradition, unable to replenish itself. Rational ethics continues its elusive search for a universal and abstract ground, but is frustrated by an ongoing disagreement within its own ranks that enables it to say more forcefully what we should not do than what we should.

All of this is not meant to suggest that we should abandon the liberal spirit, but rather that without living traditions borne by historical communities which the liberal spirit can constructively revise, it becomes empty and can only compound our confusion. We increasingly turn aimlessly in space, liberated from those historical communities that give identity and direction.

4. What, then, will supply direction for persons and societies confused by social change, historical relativity, and their liberation from concrete communities of identity and character? The affluent soci-

eties of the West propose a dominant answer from among the many possibilities. Enhance yourself. Allow your own desires to determine your direction. Those desires are close-at-hand, solid, empirical. Find the best way to make pleasurable negotiations with your environment. As the popular culture has it: Do what feels good to you. Pursue your own interest. Look out for Number One. Do it your way. Make your life an artistic statement. In the process communal bonds and the broader responsibilities they entail become secondary to the interests of the Imperial Self. The connections that tie the self to others become increasingly negotiable as the self presses for its own enhancement. More divorce, abortion, sexual exploitation, political apathy, and narrow careerism follow.

It is not that this bias toward self-centeredness is new on the human scene. Human sin has always characterized human nature. But our societies, with their affluence in the context of freedom, provide one of the few occasions in human history where masses of people have the wherewithal to pursue their desires. What is more, they can do so in a political context that ensures their liberties as long as they do not directly harm others. They can do so in a market system that responds to their every desire. The capacities for affluent people to support their self-enhancement ethic is combined with the waning certainties of traditional religious and moral claims, which have been weakened by the developments mentioned above. It may be a melancholy fact of history that people cannot handle affluence and liberty at the same time. The capability for moral self-government, which is indispensable to political and civil liberty, is eroded by the license that accompanies widespread affluence.

Confusion is inevitable in such a situation. A cultural war is going on between moral sensibilities and self-enhancement. It is not that there are no moral commitments left; it is rather that they are so mixed with the egoist impulses that are encouraged by the surrounding culture. It is never certain which directives will win out. Little can be counted on.

5. The cumulative effect of these four epochal trends is a fifth—secularization. Technical reason took the mystery out of natural processes. Historical reason debunked the claims to absoluteness that make religion tick. The liberal spirit dissolved the suprarational and the traditional by the cool light of reason. The ethic of self-enhance-

ment flowed over and obliterated the fragile demarcations of religious and moral practice. As the claims of religion weakened, so did the institution that bore them: the church. Aided by the churches' own internecine warfare and defensiveness, the forces of modernity pushed the church out of the center of the societal stage and religion out of the center of the intellectual.

The results, like those of the other four trends, are highly ambiguous. On the one hand, the world has been spared a good deal of religious conflict and bloodshed. Repressive religious lids were taken off intellectual life. Churchly controls were peeled off economics, politics, culture, and society. Tolerance increased. Human inquiry and mastery supplanted guidance by religious taboo.

But on the other hand! The world was "disenchanted." Nature lost its sacral dimension. Moral and spiritual certainties evaporated into midair. The promise of heaven and the threat of hell waned as significant sanctions. Much of what was held precious lost its ultimate legitimation and had to settle for penultimate supports. Moral motivation was cut off from its religious roots.

Above all, the meaning system projected by religion over all of life came tumbling down and the world lost its rhyme and reason. With God dead anything was possible. Humans sought to fill the vacuum produced by the departure of religion with many strange substitutes. Fascism, communism, and nationalism were pushed forward as new gods. Sensing the danger in such collective totems, much of the Western elite preferred to lead lives of either heroic existentialism or quiet skepticism. In either case, the religious factor ceased to be significant.

While ordinary people receive the signals of secularism only from afar, they are nevertheless affected, perhaps more pervasively than they think. While religion has certainly not departed as a significant factor in their lives, its long-range future is not automatically assured. Religious confusion and malaise haunt many sectors of Western societies.

Thus, the "triumphs" we have delineated are hardly that. They have their own inner contradictions. The triumph of technical reason brings along with its dominance of nature a rapid technological change that threatens the natural environment itself as well as stable human communities. Historical reason, with its deeper and wider capacities to understand our place in history and society, brings with it a debilitating sense of relativism and rudderlessness. The liberal spirit, with its confidence in Reason to supply direction in a world of historical and social relativity, finds that the moral air becomes distressingly thin as it climbs the mountain of rational enlightenment and leaves particular communities in the valley far below. Affluence carries with its promise of a better life the distinct possibility of existence characterized by chaotic desire. Secularization flattens out our existence.

Religiously speaking, these inner contradictions simply illustrate that the capacities for evil grow alongside the capacities for good. Each human achievement, like the tower of Babel, has hidden within it the propensity of humans to claim too much for it, to trust it unduly, and to ignore the evil that comes with those excesses. In other words, humans make idols of their capacities and achievements. Our confusion is much like that of Babel; we vainly think we can do more with what we have than we actually can, and when we fail we become confused and then aggressive or despondent. Twentieth-century humans repeat the idolatries of their forebears, only in different guise and form. And all of society—including the young—cast about for their bearings.

FINDING OUR BEARINGS

The first thing to be aware of in struggling with a confusing situation is that we are not without possibilities. The situation in which we live is an amazing mixture of progress and regress. Who would give up the achievements of a technological society? The possibilities it affords are breathtaking. Who would refuse the freedom that allows us to make considered choices about the values by which we want to live? Who would ignore the humility that accrues from our knowledge about our small and relative place in history and the cosmos, and exchange it for the rigid and unchastened authority of the past or, in some sad cases, the present? Who would reject the more pleasurable existence that is available to increasing numbers of people in the West?

In any fair estimation of human possibilities in history—particularly for ordinary people—this epoch in Western history is a good time to be alive. But, as I argued above, it is not without serious challenges. Above all, we need to regain more confidence and clarity in our religious and moral outlook.

An important start in regaining them is the heightened awareness among leading students of modernity that the liberal spirit and the ethic of self-enhancement cannot adequately guide personal and social life. This negative judgment is accompanied by an expectant turn toward living communities to supply that guidance. A new friendliness toward religious community is often a part of this turn.

Sociologists who are interested in broad social and cultural analysis—among them Daniel Bell, Robert Bellah, and Robert Nisbet—have identified a highly individualistic hedonism as one of the potent shapers of life in Western societies. In their view the liberal spirit does not know how to respond to the unbridled excesses of the self-enhancement ethic. In fact, it tends to exacerbate the chaos by defending the spontaneous expression of freedom, no matter what direction that expression takes. These sociologists find an appeal to science or reason unhelpful in supplying a renewed sense of direction and restraint. But they believe that religious sources are more likely able to provide help.

A number of political philosophers—such as Alasdair MacIntyre, Bernard Williams, and Michael Sandel—are likewise harsh in their assessment of the liberal spirit. The rationalistic ethics so dear to the liberal spirit is found seriously wanting in their analyses. Rather, we must return to traditions that bear a set of substantive purposes for personal and social life. These traditions, embodied in ongoing communities, carry with them the practices that enable the purposes to be reached, practices that form the character and dispositions of members of the community. There seems to be a return to Aristotle in moral and political philosophy. This means a higher evaluation of narrative-formed communities of character. Instead of relying upon some illusory universal and abstract rational capacity for self-legislation, these philosophers call for locating moral formation in communities of practice that embody particular visions of life.

Leaders in education are criticizing both the narrow notion of education as a means to make a living and the 1960s tendency to encourage students to take whatever courses they were interested in. Both perspectives undermine the coherence of education, one viewing it as an instrumentality for particular job-related purposes, the other dissolving it through the contrary tugs of "felt needs." There is a turn in philosophy of education toward insisting on a common core of the best that has been thought and written about the human condition. Even religious traditions, banished by the liberal spirit as essentially irrational, private, and contentious, are suggested as proper subjects of study in such a common core. There is an enhanced awareness that education can neglect only at its and the nation's peril the religious outlook that has crucially informed the culture of Western societies. Education cannot be "liberated" from its classical and religious foundations without itself becoming incoherent and directionless.

Developments in Christian ethics have corresponded with these trends. Christian ethics in the time from 1965 to 1980 were characterized by two emphases. First, there was an emphasis on the nature of moral reasoning and how it moves toward conclusions in particular cases. This process, while carried on by Christian ethicists, was more indebted to analytical philosophy than theology. Second, there was a great interest in particular issues—civil rights, war and peace, nuclear energy, economic philosophy, professions, medicine, sexual identity, and abortion. Ethicists explored these issues in depth, but when making judgments often either appealed to principles derived mainly from philosophy or to selected elements of religious ethics. In most of these instances, inadequate attention was given to the systematic-theological basis for Christian ethics. Furthermore, there was a rationalistic bias in these approaches in which getting principles and their applications intellectually straight was the main task of Christian ethics.

Since around 1980, however, there has been a sharp criticism of these tendencies and a movement toward more concern for the holistic theological basis of moral judgments and for the role of character and virtue in moral existence. Stanley Hauerwas has been the most publicly visible leader of this movement, though now there are many participants. This movement, along with its companion movement in theology called "narrative theology," emphasizes the crucial role of living, historical, narrative-formed communities that actually bear a religious and moral vision and practice. It rejects the search for an abstract, universal, rational base for morality, thereby conceding some of the more radical judgments of historical reason. From its point of view, there is no morality, or religion for that matter, except that of specific, historical communities. Likewise, theology and ethics, the disciplined reflection on religion and morality, are not possible without being anchored in concrete religious communities.

In a similar vein, at least formally speaking, liberation theology and ethics have turned from the earlier preoccupations of Christian ethics toward the vision and practice of historical communities. But, unlike the movement mentioned earlier, liberation theology and ethics look to the community of the oppressed for their vision and practice. For very different reasons than those of the movement described above, liberation theology likewise accepts the conclusions of historical reason, especially in its Marxist critical version, that there is no adequate universal, abstract, and rational base for Christian ethics, only the vision and practice of historical communities, particularly those involved in revolutionary practice. Again, like its narrative companions, liberation theology is highly critical, if not contemptuous, of the liberal spirit, the self-enhancement ethic, as well as the unguided trajectory of technological reason.

All of the above are examples of intellectual shifts. But most certainly the intellectual shifts reflect changes at the level of lived experience. Persons experience the quandaries of modernity that we discussed earlier, and they begin to search for their bearings amid their social and institutional existence, not merely in the intellectual currents of the day. This is most certainly true of religious people and their communities. At least some of them, whom we shall discuss later, have attempted to revivify their religious life, introduce more discipline into their moral life, and clarify their identities in the face of the confusions of the modern age. Constructive care for religious education of the young, for nurturing marriage and family bonds, for the evangelization of the unattached, and for drawing out the social-ethical implications of religious commitments have been strengthened markedly in such communities.

If these several shifts are paradigmatic of larger moves, we may be seeing a constructive address to the confusions we discussed at the beginning of this chapter. There are glimmerings of serious efforts to regain religious and moral foundations for our scientific, technological, political, economic, and educational endeavors. To use an economic metaphor, we are beginning to engage in "supply-side" strategies. As economists have argued that there must be as much attention given to the production of wealth as there is to its disposition and distribution, so many Western thinkers have come to the conclusion that our civilization is in serious need of a supply of religious and moral "capital." Historical reason has relativized and the liberal spirit has criticized and qualified the "capital" we have inherited. The self-enhancement ethic has not unexpectedly been unable to supply the commitment needed for cohesive personal and social life, including the guidance of the technological capacities we have developed. We have depleted our religious and moral capital over the centuries and now find ourselves dangerously close to bankruptcy.

But, happily enough, there has been a consciousness of the abyss toward which we have moved and an effort to regain our bearings. But doing so will be no easy task. There can be no simple return to the past with its religious and moral articulations. Historical reason has taught us too many lessons. Living traditions must constantly redefine themselves in accordance with the challenges of present and future. New occasions teach new duties. Nor can there be a hard-nosed reliance on traditional authority and power. The liberal spirit bears enough truth to prevent us from regressing to such a dangerous path. And, despite the complexities of a technological society, there can be no turning from its limits and possibilities. Regaining our bearings must take place exactly within such a situation or its efforts will turn out to be escapist or worse.

Among the religious communities that may help Christian people regain their bearings are those that share crucial characteristics. The first of those characteristics is a conviction by ordinary folk and leaders alike that their tradition points to the truth about God and his relation to humanity and the world. They have confidence in their central religious vision. This confidence is embodied in concrete religious and moral life. This seems terribly obvious, but it is nevertheless of crucial importance. Many religious traditions, buffeted by modernity and enticed by secular answers to modernity's challenges, have lost their confidence in the intrinsic truth of their religious convictions. Instead of operating out of those convictions, they adapt secular agenda and make religious beliefs and practices instrumental to those agenda.

A second characteristic is that that confidence issues in solid theological and ethical articulations of the religious community in question. The living ethos of the community is reflected in distinct theological and ethical formulations. Substantive theological and ethical concerns are not dissolved into rampant pluralism or endless methodological musings.

A third characteristic is that these communities are open to the world, not in the sense that they take their predominant direction from the world, but in the sense that they engage it dialogically. The world and its history are God's, and the challenges coming from them have to be taken in some sense as the address of the Lord of history. With such an approach, they are unlikely to foreclose too quickly on the dialogue with the world. While committed, they will also be civil, characterized by a lack of defensiveness that is the fruit of their confidence.

Who, then, are these people who will aid us in regaining our bearings, now that there is some consciousness of our confusion and a newfound openness to the claims of specific religious traditions? Who has a living, confident religious and moral ethos, a distinctive theology and ethics that reflects and supports it, and a committed yet civil openness to dialogue with the world? Contributions can be made from other sectors of the religious community, but in the following I will focus only on Christian groups, especially on those groups who can make distinctive contributions.

One of the key contributors to the process of regaining our bearings is that which is technically known as the "sectarian" option, or perhaps more acceptable to those in it, that of the "radical Reformation." This option stems from the Anabaptist movement of the sixteenth century, that part of the Reformation that believed Martin Luther and John Calvin had not gone far enough in their reforming efforts. While the Anabaptist movement was a complex phenomenon, a few distinguishing marks can be discerned among its heirs. First among these marks is a commitment to the radical teaching of Jesus as a direct, literal guide to personal and social life. When Jesus exhorts his followers to "turn the other cheek," he means just that. Such an injunction applies not only to personal life but also to social life. This means that the Christian community, if it is to be faithful to the Jesus story, must be consistently pacifist, never threatening or engaging in violence, even in self-defense.

Such teaching has generally put the followers of the radical Reformation at odds with their surrounding society. They refuse oaths of loyalty to the state and they refuse to serve in armed forces. In fact, because political power generally involves some sort of coercive power over others, followers of the radical way are unlikely to hold public office. They refuse to compromise with "the world." The crucial substance of their ethic is derived from the teaching of Jesus, not from philosophical sources. Thus they aim at a peaceable life according to New Testament teachings.

Historians of Christianity have often noted that such groups play a very important role in the interplay of Christianity and the world. Because they insist on a strict adherence to what they believe to be original biblical faith and life, they bear a very distinct identity. The Mennonites in their various shades of strictness come immediately to mind. This sharp distinction from the world around them is a constant reminder to those Christian churches and persons who are more intimately related to the world, partaking of it in various ways. The temptation of the great "church" traditions—Catholic, Lutheran, and Reformed—is to become too compromised in their involvement with the world. The "sectarians" keep the "churches" healthily off-balance by provoking constant examination of their relation to the world.

The most important theological proponent of this "sectarian" tradition has been John Howard Yoder, the Mennonite theologian and ethicist. In his *Politics of Jesus,* he not only restated the radical Reformation's commitment to the direct teaching of Jesus as a guide to social existence, he did so from within a religious community that resolutely practiced what it preached. This radical viewpoint fell upon the fertile ground of Christians who felt their own lives and the lives of their religious communities had lost Christian distinctiveness and therefore all prophetic tension with the world. Among these is Stanley Hauerwas, who was already leading the turn of Christian ethics toward a reconsideration of the role of character and virtue in Christian ethics, particularly as character and virtue are formed in the narrative-shaped community of the church. Convinced of the truthfulness of the radical Reformation's version of Christian faith and life, Hauerwas, with Yoder, has pressed forward the agenda of "sectarian" Christianity.

This is sectarianism with a difference, however. Whereas much of the radical Reformation withdrew from the world in order to live a quiet and peaceable life, this new emergence of sectarian vigor is intent on engaging the world. It is constantly in vigorous dialogue with other Christian groups and persons, raising its uncomfortable questions and proposing its stringent agenda. True enough, its engagement of the world is generally aimed at revealing to the world its true nature as world, that is, violent and coercive. Nevertheless, it does so from a perspective that has integrity and courage. It is attractive and helpful to those who are searching for their bearings in a confused world. Such an option has generated movements in many churches.

Much can be said in a similar vein about many evangelical Christians. Though churches like the Southern Baptists and a considerable number of smaller denominations do not propose such a stringent tension with the world, they have been utterly serious about maintaining a disciplined faith and life and a solid theological direction. Moreover, they are increasingly stepping forward to engage in dialogue with other churches and the world. No longer content to remain invisible and passive, they are becoming publicly relevant.

Fundamentalists are a more difficult group. While one can admire their discipline and seriousness in shaping a clear Christian faith and life, their rigidities are more perplexing. They have seemed all too ready to deny the validity of other Christian viewpoints if they depart from fundamentalism's strict codes of belief and practice. However, as conservative Protestantism has emerged from the backwaters of American life that it was sentenced to after the Scopes trial, fundamentalism has enjoyed some success in flexing its muscles. It is more confident and, to a certain extent, less defensive. This has opened at least some sectors of fundamentalism to the possibility of dialogue with other Christians and the world. This is a promising development that must be welcomed by all Christians. After all, fundamentalism affirms a good deal of the heartland of Christian belief even though it extends too much authority to doctrines that are not a part of that heartland, for example, the insistence on the plenary verbal inspiration of the Bible, and its tendency to equate debatable political policies with the "Christian" way.

One could not discuss religious resources for finding our bearings without taking into account the Roman Catholic tradition. It is so large, so varied, so resilient, and so capable of tapping many wells of strength that its vision of the Christian faith will always play a powerful role in Christian redefinition. Having had throughout the ages a powerful ethos and a disciplined theology and ethics to articulate it, the Roman Catholic Church since Vatican II is in a much more lively dialogue with the world and with other Christians. It is struggling with modernity more constructively than it has for many decades. Its bishops are relating Catholic social teachings to issues common to the whole society rather than only to those distinctively "Catholic." New and radical strands of Catholic piety bubble up as Catholic people engage in action for peace and justice. It is difficult to overestimate the role that Catholics can play in gaining our bearings.

All is not sweetness and light among Catholics, however. The great consensus generated by centuries of authority has eroded markedly, partly due to the challenges of modernity but partly due to dubious ways of meeting those challenges. It seems that Vatican II, along with its liberating possibilities, has also opened the church to many mistakes that Protestants have made earlier on. Educational and spiritual formation have been weakened. Religious and moral discipline have slackened. Confidence in central Christian affirmations has been supplanted by hopes in secular alternatives, especially those of a psychological and political nature. The cadre of ordained leadership has shrunk. With all this said, though, the remaining strength and momentum of the Catholic tradition is formidable: we will not find our bearings without Rome.

The same might be said about the old Protestant establishment—Presbyterians, Episcopalians, Methodists, and the United Church of Christ—though it would be said with a bit less conviction. The Protestant mainline was crucial in the formation of America: it shaped the great Protestant culture that in turn conditioned our education, politics, business, and social life. The mainline truly conformed to what Ernst Troeltsch called the "church type," that is, it had an intent to penetrate the surrounding culture and it had the vitality in fact to do so. A good deal of the "shaping of America" was performed by that grouping of churches. These mainline churches are now in decline, however. Their leaders and theologians seem eager to pronounce doom upon the society and culture that they had such a strong hand in shaping. While their stance is certainly open to dialogue with other churches and the world, the dialogue is less than satisfactory because their own inner identity and vitality, along with the accompanying theology and ethics, have been vitiated. Though creative theology and ethics are done, they are characterized by a diversity that leads one to worry that a sustaining tradition is no longer to be found within those churches. Without at least one foot in a living tradition it is all too easy to take signals from secular trends. While there are calls from the grass roots to reconnect with the older streams of mainline tradition, it remains to be seen whether this can or will happen. But certainly the Protestant mainstream cannot be written off as Christians struggle to regain their footing.

This brings us to the last grouping in our discussion, the Lutherans. Lutherans have always been somewhat difficult to categorize, at least on the American scene. Lutherans have been too Protestant to identify as Catholics, and too Catholic to identify as Protestants. Indeed, they tend to view themselves as evangelical Catholics. They have not been part of the great Protestant mainline that has shaped America; until recently they remained in rather isolated ethnic enclaves. Though isolated from public life, they have not been "sectarian" in orientation, as described above. Though focused on the Bible, they have not in the main been literalistic in the fundamentalist sense. They are something of a curious lot.

Lutherans have a strong, discernible religious and moral ethos grounded in a large number of people, perhaps seven to eight million in North America. Carrying on a rich tradition of theological and biblical study from their northern European forebears, they articulate a clear and constructive theology and ethic. And, despite their ethnic character, they have for the most part been pioneers in ecumenical dialogue and have striven to engage American culture. We should not be too sanguine about Lutherans, however. They have not been terribly successful in breaking out of their ethnic and geographical bastions. Because of this, they have declined along with the decline in immigration from northern Europe. In some ways they imitate their compatriots in mainline Protestantism, allowing secular trends in American society to dictate too much of their style and substance. Their momentum has waned, much like that of establishment Protestantism. Nevertheless, they are a large body with rich traditions of worship, theology, and ethics. They will have much to contribute, even as it is hoped that this book is a part of that contribution.

WHY THESE BEARINGS?

An important question to be dealt with at this point concerns our opting for a religious route to finding our bearings, particularly a Christian religious route. After all, there are other options. One can continue the Enlightenment trust in science and reason as the way of discerning who we are, where we are going, and what we ought to be doing. Or, one can give up any hope of finding one's bearings, as a few have done in the intellectual sphere and many in the practical sphere of day-to-day living. Or, one can look for answers among other world religions, the occult, or some idiosyncratic mixture of all these outlooks. Why the Christian religious answer?

For the most part, the reader will have to read the rest of the book to discern whether my delineation of the Christian life is persuasive or not. Without presuming to justify fully the Christian religious option, however, I would like to offer a few general reasons for my choice.

First, it is important to make an empirical point. Among all the organizations on the face of the earth in which persons voluntarily participate (that excludes the nation-state), the Christian church in all its various parts must be the largest. It has sustained its faith and life for almost two thousand years. Moreover, it continues to grow. In America it dwarfs all other voluntary activities. What other organization can claim to have over 40 percent of the population in its activities at a given hour in the week? What other nonprofit organization can elicit the financial support that the churches do? What other organization provides as much spiritual and moral nurture, care, and direction?

These rhetorical questions are posed for two reasons, one negative and one positive. Negatively, they are put and answered to challenge the widespread underestimation of the churches' empirical weight by those among the educational and intellectual elite of our country who are pervasively secularist in orientation. One can wade through books on contemporary moral issues without coming across any mention of the Christian churches' influence on countless moral agents whose moral sentiments are decisively conditioned by that influence. It is as if religion were hermetically sealed off from daily life. Religion appears in this view to be a private, irrational affair of Sunday while quite another drummer determines the beat for life from Monday through Saturday. This is emphatically not the case, however; which brings us to the positive thrust of our answers. The Christian churches nurture an ethos that powerfully shapes the whole life of their people. A world view is proffered, one that conveys content about the ultimate context in which we live, move, and have our being. The nature of the world and of history, of the human predicament and its salvation, and of human obligation in the light of all this are sketched out as part of that world view. The biblical narratives and the theological reflection upon them, aided by the science and philosophy of the day, provide that sketch. While this sketch is not a photograph that can be entered as hard evidence in a scientific investigation, it is a reasonable effort to grasp the contours of ultimacy that lie beyond and beneath human science as we know it.

These cognitive elements are not confined in wooden, textbook propositions. They are rehearsed and celebrated in worship and music, preaching and education, prayer and meditation. These activities elicit affections of gratitude and praise, repentance and joy in forgiveness, obligation, and hope *from* those who participate and *toward* that One to which all the religious symbols and activities point. There is a rich emotional texture woven around the Christian vision, and both the vision and its affective responses are open to a wide spectrum of persons, not just the educated elite.

Finally, this large and living Christian ethos shapes the will of Christian persons. Intentions of service toward others, and the moral habits of character that enable such service, are cultivated in many of the practices of the community. Christian churches are communities of moral character and virtue.

In short, one strong reason for looking to Christian religious communities for help in gaining our bearings is that they are already doing so for a great portion of the population. They may not be doing so as persuasively and extensively as we might wish, but nevertheless the job is being done.

Such an appeal to empirical reality is not finally persuasive, however. Claims to truth are not adjudicated by appeals to the quantity of people involved nor even to the longevity of the group, though both criteria have some weight. Rather, we must make a deeper claim, which runs as follows: the central affirmations of the Christian faith correspond with the deepest aspirations of the human spirit for a meaningful world, personal significance, affirmation and forgiveness, moral purpose, and hope for the future. That to which the Christian faith points fulfills the most profound human longing. As Augustine wrote: "Our hearts are restless until they are at home with Thee." The God revealed in Christ, so the Christian claim goes, is the source of meaning, human significance, moral purpose, and hope. While the Christian faith is the human response to that revelation and therefore inevitably flawed and partial, it nevertheless is a vessel that points to that God.

Such an argument is of course open to several objections. The first is that these affirmations are simply human projections. Humans indeed have the aspirations mentioned above, and have invented marvelous systems of meaning—religion—to fulfill those needs. In this view religion has an important function but certainly no claim to truth. A second objection is that such a view of religion subordinates God's will to human needs and aspirations. God is expected to meet human desires, thereby becoming an instrument of human will. God is no longer the center; humans are. The deity of God is radically qualified. In both objections, religion becomes an instrument for fulfilling human needs, in the former case as an invention of cosmic comfort without a real referent, in the latter a blasphemous displacement of God's transcendent intentions for quite human immanent purposes.

To the former objection we admit that the Christian meaning system is indeed a human projection. But the real question is whether or not it is a *true* projection, that is, whether or not it corresponds with the ultimate ground from which it arises. It may be true that the human quest correlates with the ultimate truth. That at least is what the Christian claim is. The matching-up between aspiration and true fulfillment is performed by the Christian revelation. This match-up is then evidenced by human experience, reason, and the extensity and duration of the claim. That is what we shall argue as we proceed later to our explication of the Christian life.

To the latter, the objection that the fulfillment of human concerns has displaced God as the center of Christian faith, two responses can be made. First, the heart of the Christian faith—its good news—is that God has pursued lost humanity. The miracle is that God has shown himself to be friendly and gracious. We insignificant specks, and disobedient ones at that, are objects of the Divine Love. It is clear that such a message is open to many distortions but that does not make the central proclamation any less wonderful or true. Second, the gospel affirms that such a demonstration of Divine Love occurs only through vicarious suffering. The rescue of humankind is not achieved without great cost. The cross is a constant reminder of the cost of God's rescue mission. Such a message confounds human expectation and calculation. It does not flow smoothly from human wants and desires. At least it did not for those who met the historical Jesus with misunderstanding and, finally, rejection and betrayal. It demands of us a humble and penitent heart, the trusting acceptance of God's grace, and a new life of servanthood to all. The road to life leads through the narrow passage. Our immediate and distorted desires are burned away in this narrow passage so that deeper and purer aspirations might emerge and be fulfilled.

Thus, we can say that God's revelation both fulfills and contradicts human expectations. But its fulfillment of our deeper longings evidences the fact that God's truth cannot and does not finally contradict the deeper aspirations of the creatures of God, for those aspirations have been built into the creation by the Creator.

Even though we might claim that Christian truth is corroborated by the deepest levels of human experience and enlightened reason, there is a sense in which we cannot escape human relativity. We are operating from within the circle of faith. Though we do not doubt the reality of what we see through our historical spectacles, we are quite aware that those spectacles are distorted by our involvement in time and history. We see through a glass darkly. We must confess what we see, act with integrity from what we see, and leave the final judgment to God.

Efforts at finding our bearings will be particularized in this book even beyond the Christian option. They will be shaped by Christian convictions in their Lutheran interpretation. Besides being a Lutheran by birth and nurture, I am one by continuing conviction. My primary reason is that I find the Lutheran tradition to be thoroughly and consistently evangelical, and therefore it points to what is most uniquely Christian. It has articulated and preserved in each succeeding generation God's good news, the evangel. This is the surprising, wondrous news of God's graciousness. God has worked out our salvation for us in Christ. Redemption is offered freely and unconditionally; we need only accept God's grace. Upon receiving God's gift we are enabled by the Spirit to conform ourselves more closely to God's intentions in the world, but that activity *follows* from that grace and does not earn it, elicit it, or even cooperate with it. It is free.

That great gift can be best understood and appreciated in the context of a most realistic and profound reading of the human predicament, in both its height and depth. The Lutheran tradition grasps both the sublimity of God's grace and the height and depth of the human predicament in both its personal and social dimensions. It therefore catches the paradoxical nature of our condition in the world and of God's response to that condition. This radical message of grace—justification by grace through faith on account of Christ—is therefore surrounded by correlative teachings that both guard and express this radical message and its paradoxical relation to human existence in a fallen world. Teachings concerning the nature of Christian liberty, the twofold way that God rules the world, and especially concerning the calling of the Christian in daily life are examples of these correlative doctrines. This Lutheran framework will pervade the argument of the book, which will be discernible to all those familiar with that tradition. It should be added that it is a Lutheran framework that has been engaged by other Christian traditions and perspectives. The contemporary ecumenical conversation can enrich every particular religious tradition.

THE PLAN OF THE BOOK

Given the analysis of the current situation at the beginning of this chapter, a focus limited to ethics would be insufficient. The problem in this time of confusion is not simply "what ought we to do," but also "who are we" and "what is going on." One cannot deal with the latter two questions without developing something of the theological ground for Christian ethics. Theology, reflecting on the faith of the Christian community, articulates who we are and what is going on in the world. It aims at saying something meaningful about our identity—who, or perhaps better, whose we are. It cannot say anything about our identity as human beings, however, except by relating us to the larger context in which we exist. Theology therefore attempts descriptions of the world and what is going on in it. In brief, this book addresses our being as well as our doing, the constitution of our identity as well as that identity in action. It aims at developing an interpretation of the Christian life.

The first part will deal with our identity, our being-in-the-world. It is entitled "The Call of God," for it is the ceaseless and relentless call of God that bestows meaning and identity upon us. We will discuss the initiative of God and the nurture of Christian being. The second part will deal with "The Calling of the Christian." It is in the Christian calling, the vocation of the Christian, that Christian being becomes active. Christian identity issues forth in action. Christian doing also affects Christian being, however; the two poles interact. Our identities are shaped by our responsibilities. This second part will deal with the *general* notion of Christian calling. It will examine the general nature of responsibility, moral development, and the elements of Christian consciousness that transform worldly responsibility into an authentic vocation or calling. Part 3 will focus on the calling*s* of the Christian. It will probe the *specific* spheres in which Christians act out their vocation—marriage and family life, work, public life, and life in the church. Part 3 will deal with the proper principles and practices for each of these spheres, and with how specifically Christian moral notions interact with them.

BIBLIOGRAPHY

On cultural and moral fragmentation:

Bell, Daniel. *The Cultural Contradictions of Capitalism.* New York: Basic Books, 1976.

Bellah, Robert. *Habits of the Heart: Individualism and Commitment in American Life.* Berkeley and Los Angeles: University of California Press, 1985.

MacIntyre, Alasdair. *After Virtue: A Study in Moral Theology.* 2d ed. Notre Dame, Ind.: University of Notre Dame Press, 1984.

Nisbet, Robert. *Twilight of Authority.* New York and London: Oxford University Press, 1975.

On criticisms of liberalism:

MacIntyre. *After Virtue.*

Sandel, Michael. *Liberalism and the Limits of Justice.* New York and Cambridge: Cambridge University Press, 1982.

Williams, Bernard. *Ethics and the Limits of Philosophy.* Cambridge: Harvard University Press; London: Fontana Books, 1985.

On the role of character and virtue:

Hauerwas, Stanley. *Character and the Christian Life: A Study in Theological Ethics.* San Antonio: Trinity University Press, 1985.

———. *The Peaceable Kingdom: A Primer in Christian Ethics.* Notre Dame, Ind.: University of Notre Dame Press, 1983.

———. *Vision and Virtue: Essays in Christian Ethical Reflection.* Notre Dame, Ind.: University of Notre Dame Press, 1986.

On liberation theology:

Cone, James. *A Black Theology of Liberation.* Philadelphia: J. B. Lippincott Co., 1970; 2d ed., Maryknoll, N.Y.: Orbis Books, 1986.

Gutiérrez, Gustavo. *A Theology of Liberation.* Maryknoll, N.Y.: Orbis Books, 1972.

Russell, Letty. *Human Liberation in a Feminist Perspective: A Theology.* Philadelphia: Westminster Press, 1974.

By a modern representative of the "radical Reformation":

Yoder, John Howard. *The Politics of Jesus.* Grand Rapids: Wm. B. Eerdmans, 1972.

On the social role of the church:

Niebuhr, H. Richard. *The Kingdom of God in America.* New York: Harper & Brothers, 1959.

Troeltsch, Ernst. *The Social Teaching of the Christian Churches.* 2 vols. Chicago: University of Chicago Press, 1981.

On a radically theocentric perspective:

Gustafson, James M. *Ethics from a Theocentric Perspective.* Vol. 1, *Theology and Ethics.* Chicago: University of Chicago Press, 1981.

PART
I

THE CALL OF
GOD

Fear not, for I have redeemed you;
I have called you by name, you are mine.
                    (Isaiah 43:1)

In the continuing confusion of our world God continues to call all persons even though many refuse to listen or respond. God calls us particularly through the testimony of peoples—first Israel and then the church—who have witnessed his mighty acts. They have mediated the call of God which was addressed first to them and through them to us. The Holy Scriptures are the primary vehicle of God's address, but the history of the Christian church is a continuing witness to the Word of God.

While the address of God to us was decisively and fully realized in Jesus as the Christ, God continues to speak in historical events, personal experiences, and nature. Though these "words" are always ambiguous and must be validated and interpreted according to the central revelation of Jesus Christ, they are corroborations of God's continuing intentions to call his people.

The following two chapters examine how God continues to call us, and how, once we listen to that call, his Spirit nurtures our responses.

2

The Divine Initiative

But you are a chosen race, a royal priesthood, a holy nation, God's own people, that you may declare the wonderful deeds of him who called you out of darkness into his marvelous light.

(1 Peter 2:9)

THE UNRECOGNIZED PRESENCE

From a Christian point of view, we are immersed in God. God is the hot furnace of creative love out of which all things come and to which all things go. God is the sustainer of the microcosmic processes that run the cosmos—the quarks, electrons, protons, and neutrons. He is the orderer that assures their persisting patterns. He is the ground of all the interdependencies that hold us into being and that set our limits and provide our possibilities. God is the dynamic force that moves the past into the present and the present into the future. God upholds the unfolding patterns among beings whose honoring brings peace but whose violation brings pain and suffering. He gives us life, holds us within it, and then pulls us out. He is as close to us as our breath yet more distant than can be imagined. In short, God is Creator, Sustainer, and Judge. And while our experience of God is ambiguous, the Jewish and Christian conviction is that all this activity issues from the plenitude of his being, from his lovingkindness. God is trustworthy; we can stay afloat as we live in him.

Yet we do not believe; we do not trust. Most humans upon the

earth do not acknowledge the Giver of Life with praise and thanksgiving. Many of those who do "name the name" live in contradiction
to their confession. As all other generations of humankind, we are
lost and confused in our own darkness. The modern age—which we
portrayed in chapter 1—may compound our confusion, but it certainly did not give birth to it. The biblical story of the Fall locates its
origin fast upon the heels of our creation. We rebelled and turned
away from God in our second breath of life. Murder, shame, toil,
expulsion, and death follow. The confusion of Babel is a fitting
capstone for humanity's disol⎵ ⌐ient pride. Yet God sustains us even
when we fail to acknowledge him.

It is true, though, as historians of religion tell us, that from the
beginning humans have searched for God. They have sought, and
continue to seek, a connection with the source of life and being. So
they knew many gods, each god pointing to and guaranteeing some
valuable element of reality. Fertility, power, love, wisdom, and peace
all had their divine guarantors. In their worship certain aspects of the
divine mystery were grasped—its tremendous and fascinating power.

But religious life was, and is, plagued by confusion. The many and
varied gods clash. They pull the loyal worshiper apart. So there are
attempts to place one god above others, but we can never agree which
one it shall be. Moderns continue the great tradition of human
polytheism by furtively pursuing lives partially committed to the
potencies of this and that—sex, comfort, family, achievement, nation, power, or security. Sometimes they try to elevate one above the
other but that one does not carry the freight of their aspirations for
long. The big and little gods, once bright, fade in their twilight.

This is an unusual way to talk about the lives of modern people.
Many moderns would not understand "God language" applied to
dimensions of life they would consider very "secular." And they
have a point. The world has been "disenchanted" by the processes
we discussed in chapter 1. Furthermore, modern people are encom-
passed by contemporary events that are viewed from a natural, secular perspective. Wars are the results of human conflicts. Natural
disasters are understood according to natural causes. Accidents are
attributed to human error. Economic dislocations are explained by
experts in economic science. Mental disturbances are referred to psy-
chologists. Moderns have by and large exorcised the "ghost in the
machine."

Nevertheless, in the midst of the confusion of competing values, a flattened-out, mundane consciousness, and a backdrop of possible historical disaster, God continues to call us, just as he has called humans from the beginning. God calls us with the same initiating love that called Abraham, who stands at the very beginning of God's conversation with us.

THE BIBLICAL STORY

Abraham responded to God's call to be his own people, to live in the way he willed, and to fulfill his errand in history. Out of the confusion of many divine voices, the One spoke clearly. Abraham answered and the story of God's long conversation with his people began. Blessed to be a blessing, Israel was called forth.

We know how the story goes. The people of Israel were enslaved by the pharaohs of Egypt. But with a mighty hand the Lord freed them from oppression. Through his servant Moses, God led them through the wilderness and showed them a clearer record of his will. The Law, a gracious gift of God, showed how his people would live in harmony with God and others. Peace would result from fidelity to God's sovereign will. The people, responsive to the great call, would become a beacon to the nations, an example of humans living as they were meant to live.

Wandering in a wilderness toward the promised land, the people of Israel were beset by many challenges and temptations. Harassed by external threats of other peoples and constantly tempted to follow other gods, Israel repeatedly lost faith in the Lord and was disobedient. So the journey to the promised land took many years. The Lord would not allow them to enter it until they were a fit instrument for God's purposes.

The people finally entered and were guided first by judges and then kings. The covenant made with Abraham, and reaffirmed by Jacob and Isaac, was appropriated in the new circumstances of the kingdoms of Israel. Constantly chided by the prophets, Israel struggled to keep its covenant with God. Kingdoms were shaped according to the Law and holy cities founded. The call of God, first answered by a small clan, had now brought forth a whole people. That people, as it reflected its life before God, developed profound accounts of God's creation of all that is. They chronicled and interpreted their history as an ongoing conversation with God. They developed all sorts of literature—poems, songs, wise sayings—to express their theocentric faith.

Human capacities for sin did not go away, however. Kings fell away from the way of God. The people sought other gods and neglected the way of life they were taught. The poor were oppressed and the rich became decadent. Great prophets like Amos and Hosea held up to people the demand of God. They pronounced words of harsh judgment and called for repentance. Failing this, the prophets warned, the wrath of God would be visited upon the people.

And it was. The kingdoms broke apart and gradually succumbed to their enemies. Key segments of the people were taken to Babylonia. But God did not end the conversation with his people. Prophets of hope, not judgment, arose among the exiled folk. They promised a return to the holy land and a new beginning. That new beginning was to be instigated by a fresh version of God's call. Its contours were as yet unclear but expectations were nevertheless enhanced.

Upon return, difficulties again arose quickly. The prophets' powerful insight into human sin was confirmed by continued confusion and disobedience. The great prophetic question was posed. In the light of the habitual unfaith and disloyalty of even the called and chosen people of God, can there be anything more than judgment and wrath in history?

As fragmentation and oppression by new enemies progressed, hope for something decisively new arose. In view of the unlikelihood of saving themselves on their own, people expected a savior. It was always a savior according to their own expectations. Some wanted a political liberator who would throw out the Romans and reestablish the kingdoms of Israel. Some wanted a leader who would reestablish the Temple and fidelity to the Law. Others wanted a purified and ascetic version of Jewish faith. Even the wider world outside of Israel was crackling with religious expectation. The era seemed to be a turning point in history, though there were a variety of views about what direction it would take.

A new incursion of God into history was necessary. A new and more decisive call was required. In the confusion and expectation of the time, that incursion occurred. This time, so the Christian confession goes, God was incarnated in his call. God's Word became flesh. The Eternal One dwelt among us as flesh and blood.

In the life, ministry, death, and resurrection of Jesus as the Christ Christians see the decisive fulfillment of God's loving initiative. God reached out with his own flesh and blood for a lost and confused creation. God sought a new covenant with us. He continued to love us though we had made ourselves unlovable.

Christians see in the event of Jesus Christ a double movement—a movement from humankind toward God and a movement of God toward humanity. Christian tradition holds that Jesus was the Second Adam. Whereas the First Adam fell away from God in disobedience, Jesus as the Second Adam exemplified a return to full obedience. Jesus was the epitome of monotheistic piety. He loved God with all his heart, soul, and mind and loved his neighbors with God's love. He embodied moral and spiritual virtue, and he did so within the conditions of human existence. He re-presents to God our full human possibility.

Jesus, as the Christ, is also the movement of God toward humans. As such he reveals and demonstrates the character and intentions of God toward sinful humans. Besides providing enlightenment about God, however, he *performs* salvific acts that free us from sin and death and reconciles us to God. These acts, focused in Jesus' death and resurrection, are the pivotal moment in history. They overcome the alienation of humanity from God and forge a new covenant with his people. And God does this in Jesus purely out of his graciousness for our benefit. God does it from his side of the great gap; God crosses over.

First, what does Jesus reveal about God? He reveals the sharpness and intensity of God's demand on us. Jesus announces the breaking-in of the kingdom of God and calls for repentance (turning around). He awakens our need for repentance by dramatizing the stringency of God's will. God demands purity of heart. We must cast all our trust upon him and not place that trust in lesser things. We are to love our neighbors with an unrelenting love, forgiving them seventy times seven. The powerful, wealthy, and religiously proud are particular objects of Jesus' challenge.

Jesus calls his followers to live in a way befitting God's coming rule. Taken alone, this dimension of Jesus' teaching comes as bad news, not good news. Jesus stands in the long line of lively Jewish prophets, only he radicalizes the demand of God even more than they do. God demands radical obedience, both inwardly and outwardly. However, at the same time that Jesus raises the ante with regard to God's demand upon us, he paradoxically assures us of God's unconditional love for us, in spite of our failure to live up to that demand.

In moving parables such as those about the Prodigal Son, the Lost Coin, and the Good Shepherd, Jesus points to the forgiving love of God for those who have repentant hearts and throw themselves upon the gracious mercy of God. The remorseful sinner is loved even though the sin is rejected. While we are enjoined to go and sin no more, the dominant note in the stories is God's unwavering love for us sinners. We only have to accept that love. Then in grateful joy we will renew our efforts to do God's will. But the indicative—you are affirmed, loved, forgiven—precedes the imperative: therefore go and do the will of your Father who is in heaven.

Such insights are not only taught; they are demonstrated in acts of unconditional kindness. Outsiders like tax collectors and prostitutes are included in Jesus' love. Women are affirmed. The poor are cared for. Sinners are loved and healed. Failure and betrayal are forgiven. Children are tenderly invited into his arms.

This double-edged teaching and ministry had appropriately double-edged effects. Some, particularly the lost, the outsiders, and the least, welcomed Jesus as the long-expected Messiah. They expected him to overturn the powerful and give them their proper place in the kingdom. Others who were challenged and threatened by his teaching and ministry were offended enough to begin conspiring to get rid of such a disturbing fellow.

His offensiveness was compounded when he began teaching that he, the announcer of the coming kingdom of God, must go up to Jerusalem in a public ministry to suffer and die. Even his followers could not accept that. Further, his teaching and action hinted that the expected one of God must take on the form of a servant, one who suffers and dies for others. Moreover, he claimed before religious authorities who thought distinctively differently that he and his teachings would be vindicated by God in a decisive way.

So, we might summarize his teachings and ministry in this way. He announces the rapid in-breaking of the kingdom of God. Its coming demands repentance and radical obedience. For those who hear the announcement with their hearts as well as their ears, God's unconditional affirmation and forgiveness are theirs. They can look with gladness and hope toward the full realization of God's kingdom. He, Jesus, is the clarion call of God.

In all this, Christians affirm, God reveals himself as the bringer of a kingdom ruled by unconditional love. It is a kingdom of peace and love. God is decisively calling forth his people. God speaks his Word. His call brings forth repentance, faith, obedience, and hope from those who respond.

This is not the end of the story. If it stopped here there would have been no Christian faith. Jesus would have had enough continuity with the Jewish tradition either to reform it or be absorbed by it. No, the story proceeds first of all to a bitter defeat. Jesus does in fact go to Jerusalem to complete his public ministry. After an ironic "triumphal entry" he is engaged by all who have been disappointed or offended by his teaching and his claims. And that is about everyone. As the screws are turned on him, his support falls away. His most loyal followers disappear.

He comes to a nasty end. He is crucified on orders from a Roman governor who gutlessly responds to the clamor of a mob incited by the religious authorities. Defeat and sadness reign. On the third day after his crucifixion, however, his tomb is found to be empty. His risen form appears to many of his followers. Black Friday has become Easter Sunday. He is arisen!

THE CHURCH'S STORY

What does all this mean? As Jesus' followers gathered themselves into joyous and hopeful communities of devotion, they told stories about him, reenacted his last supper with them, recounted his teachings, and reflected on the meaning of the whole event—including his crucifixion and resurrection. Writers began to gather all these materials and order them into coherent accounts and into interpretations of the meaning of these astounding but confusing events.

The era of the church had begun. The Holy Spirit, drawing together and working through these little bands, brought events and meaning together. This Jesus who proclaimed the coming of the kingdom *is* the kingdom come. The preacher became the preached.

In the events of his death and resurrection, the early Christian community saw far more than a radical Jewish prophet come to a typically persecuted end.

In those events, they recognized the liberating acts of God. Jesus of Nazareth becomes Jesus the Christ, the Savior. God in Christ has done something totally new. Besides revealing himself in a clear and decisive way, God in Christ has done what is necessary to reconcile a lost and disobedient humanity to him. God makes possible at-one-ment, atonement. He makes a new covenant with us through Christ's work.

It was difficult for the faithful community to express this cosmic drama in terms understood by earthbound mortals. So they used multiple images of Jesus as Redeemer, Justifier, Sacrifice, Savior, and Victor to grasp the meaning of what had been wrought in those mighty acts. As usual, human efforts to clarify were limited by the time and place of the clarifiers. A variety of interpretations of the Christ-event are present in the New Testament. But all of them conspire to present Christ and his work of salvation.

These interpretations hold in common that Christ is both our and God's representative in God's struggle to overcome that which separates us from him. Sin, death, and the devil are defeated in the death and resurrection of Christ. God's saving efforts have worked through the event of Christ. He has drawn near, suffered with and for us, and has emerged victorious.

This is the good news: God has entered our history as one of us, revealed his innermost intentions of love for us, and realized those intentions in a deed of suffering love. God has taken into himself the judgment and wrath owed a rebellious creation. Even God cannot simply cancel out that judgment and wrath. The effects of violating the spiritual and moral order of the world are real and must be absorbed by someone. They are absorbed by God himself through his son. God's mercy transcends his judgment, but only at great cost to him.

And our representative, Jesus, who is also God's representative, is the worker of this deed. Because he was faithful unto death in carrying through this work, God has raised him up. As victor over sin and death he is the firstborn of the dead. Those that trust in him and his work participate in his death and resurrection. He has brought it off!

It took the early communities considerable time and effort to interpret what had happened. In the New Testament we have the early church's account of Jesus' life, death, and resurrection as well as its varied reflections on the meaning of it all. The unique vocation of Jesus as the Christ is discerned. As God's decisive Word and Act, Jesus both contradicted and fulfilled human expectations of the Messiah. God's liberating act refused to conform to our notions that God would simply cooperate with our efforts to save ourselves, be those efforts through our own righteousness, our own revolutionary programs, or our own profound knowledge. Jesus dissociated himself from all those efforts. Rather, God elected to save us out of his pure grace, demanding no saving work from us. Jesus suffers on our account and invites us to participate in God's kingdom free of guilt-ridden efforts to earn that participation. How wonderful of God to choose such a way, yet how necessary! For any other route would simply allow us to change God's work into some distorted image of our own.

Though pressed by challenge from without and dissension from within, the church flourished. God's call had proceeded from one man, Abraham, and brought forth a great nation of twelve tribes. Through a chastening process the call is narrowed down to One man again, but One who makes all the difference. Through the promptings of the Holy Spirit working in another Twelve, a new nation is born, the Christian church, the body of Christ.

The early stages of the history of the church were characterized by ongoing struggles to define the parameters of the catholic faith. God's Word needed to be clarified from the human side, as it were. And it was. The canon was set, creeds agreed upon, organization constructed, worship given form. Intense faith swept through the expectant nations, beginning with the poor and ordinary folk but soon reaching the elite. Spiritual and moral qualities in the Christian communities gave them staying power in spite of persecution.

The spiritual vitality of Christianity bubbled up from below while the pagan Roman Empire crumbled from above. After Constantine, the church supplied the cohesion and direction for the civilized Western world and it sent missions to the uncivilized. It increasingly penetrated the economic, political, intellectual, moral, spiritual, and social life of the West. The West became Christendom. The church had decisively shaped its environment. God's call was extended to millions.

Such dominant power was bound to be open to corruption, however. The church became much enamored of its own secular power. It also began to claim that its own system of spiritual enrichment was the agent of human salvation, not God's free grace.

The Reformation came as a corrective to a powerful but erring church. Luther rediscovered, though it had never been fully lost, the good news of God's free grace in Christ. We are justified by grace through faith on account of Christ. God's gracious Word to us was again clarified. God's call was again clearly heard. Layers of intermediaries and regimens of work were cleared away so that the direct address of God could be received.

This break with Rome initiated by Martin Luther was followed by many others. John Calvin, Henry VIII, Ulrich Zwingli, the Anabaptists, and others broke away. The unity of the church, never fully realized even in the West, was further shattered. The fragmentation of the church, though accompanied by the release of many Protestant vitalities, is a development which has never been satisfactorily reversed.

As the Old World gained advantages in technologies of travel and warfare, it "discovered" and subdued many parts of the New. Along with the explorers, soldiers, and settlers came the Christian faith. Through highly ambiguous vehicles, God's call was extended.

Colonists came to the shores of North America—Pilgrim and Puritan, Anglican and Catholic, Lutheran and Anabaptists among them. Christian settlements proliferated and spread west, sometimes offering Native Americans a place at the table, but more often casting them aside. Enslaved black people were forcibly inducted into the faith in the South. But again the churches flourished and America became a "Christian" land.

It was through the German pioneers of Nebraska, cared for by Lutheran missionary pastors, that the call of God came to my forebears and to me.

MY STORY

I heard the call of God to be his own in a very normal and unexciting way. My parents were not particularly religious. They were very young when I was born toward the end of the Depression. But when they had a youngster on their hands they brought him for Baptism right after birth, and to Sunday school at an early age. At the same time they began to increase their attachments to and activities in the church. In our little all-German town, you were either Lutheran or Catholic. Those churches spent considerable effort on the formation of their young. Sunday schools were large and in ours a common assembly was held before we were sent to our specific classes. Mrs. Thompson led the assembly with rousing gospel songs that owed more to the Methodist movement on the frontier than our own Lutheran tradition of hymnody. I know those gospel songs by the hundreds.

We preschoolers wailed when we were promoted from our comfortable little room where Jesus' disputation with the elders peered down on us from among the steam pipes. Kindly teachers told us the Christian story and embodied Christian virtue through their loyalty, forbearance, and affection for children. In later high-school years teachers were even intellectually stimulating. One, Mrs. Beckenhauer, bet me a milkshake that humans would be able to control the weather in twenty years. I collected my winnings years ago.

Sunday school was always followed by compulsory attendance at church in the large nave above the Sunday-school rooms. There the call of God was deeply etched into my consciousness. The moods of the church year, closely intertwined with the seasons, are yet instantly retrievable to my memory. The expectation of Advent with its wreath and candles. The pristine winter purity of Christmas; Mrs. Hasebroock singing "Star of the East" at the midnight candlelight communion. The somberness of Lent—no movies but plenty of midweek services. The triumphant spring of souls—Easter. On through the long season of Trinity with its strong preaching by Pastor Krebs.

Confirmation brought a vivid encounter with the Holy Spirit, which was palpably present as we took our first Holy Communion in white robes. That time was also appropriate for getting serious about the Christian life. One was to become a model Christian in life outside the church. The Christian way was starkly clear and sometimes at painful odds with the ways of the world. Though they were legalistic and tempted to self-righteousness, those deeds were still efforts at Christian virtue.

A particularly important part of my early formation as a Christian was the experience of a "call to the ministry," as it was termed in those days. This had not only to do with who (or whose) I was as a child of God, but also with what I should do with my life.

Now the last thing I wanted to do with my life was become a pastor. Pastors were "unmanly" and definitely not a model for young athletes, which I tried to be. Most of my "heroes" were athletes and coaches. Men were devout Christians in our church and town, but religion was never talked about nor were one's religious "affections" ever worn on one's sleeve. Pastors did both and, while respected for their necessary leadership, were not particularly to be emulated.

Against these odds a strange thing happened while I was working as a gardener for one of the most prestigious and well-educated women in our church. I overheard her talking on the phone with one of her friends. During the conversation she opined that indeed that Bobby Benne would make an excellent minister. I was nailed! After that "word" I was never able completely to shake the notion that I was cut out to be a full-time worker in the church. That "call" came against most of my surface inclinations. After it, however, I secretly prepared for the kind of course work and college program that conventionally led toward ordination.

The call of God to be his own and to do his bidding came to me through the church in that particular time and place. The orderliness and reliability conveyed by that early formation in the faith have communicated a sense of trust deeper than mere intellectual assent. Faith and life fit together hand and glove. In spite of absurdities and painful setbacks, life—and the power behind it—is basically for us and not against us. One can have a basic confidence in things. God is our rock.

That early faith did not lack a sense of sin. Though rather legalistically conceived, our notion of sin convinced us that we were disobedient sinners. We needed the forgiveness offered by God in Christ. So we came with repentant hearts to the Lord's Supper. Receiving forgiveness, we resolved to live upright lives—sexual restraint, soberness, honesty, and hard work—and to be charitable and kindly to those less fortunate than we. For me those less fortunate were particularly the "oddballs" in our school who were not athletes, good-looking, or popular. I tried to befriend a number of them in order to lessen a bit their sense of isolation.

Formation in the faith also meant that one was here on earth for a purpose, that is, to do God's will in one's work. One was not simply here to enjoy oneself or to support one's family, but to discern what it was that God wanted you to do and then do it as best you could.

Finally, there was a sense of gratitude for the fact that life was as good as it was. We were not raised on high expectations and we were constantly surprised that eventualities outran expectations. One praised God for those blessings and faced the future with a modicum of hope.

This simple posture of Christian faith and life was "caught" from the adults of family and church. The practice of the Christian faith and life in that place shaped my character and outlook powerfully. The dependencies of our early life "make" us what we are to a much greater extent than we would like to admit. When those dependencies are shaped by those who are also formed by the Christian story by their forebears, they can well be counted as God's special gifts to us.

Formation in the church was certainly not the only conditioner of my life. As for most other people, the immediate family was as powerful, if not more. Parents from Nebraska farms and small towns bore strong virtues of the frontier. Self-reliance, uncomplaining endurance, loyalty, and compassion for the "deserving" poor and unfortunate were emphasized. Above all, "doing the best one can" was prized. This trait was most vividly admired in athletes, but for me it quickly got channeled into academics and music as well.

Such an upbringing blossomed under the conditions of small-town Nebraska life. There the American Dream was a reality. We were free to shake off the limits of the past, to engage in a struggling ascent, and to live in confident hope that such efforts would be embraced by a gracious future. The land and society were open.

Everyone started from roughly the same starting point and the rules of the game were generally fair. One could rise according to ability, choice, and ambition. In the distinctly human scale of the small town, one could participate in a wide variety of activities— drama, debate, sports of each season, vocal and instrumental music, journalism, scouts—as well as the prescribed schooling. Since it was such a small pond, "excellence" was not reserved for specialists, but was accessible to the relatively gifted and strongly motivated generalist. Such an environment breeds an appreciation for the variety of life's activities, a thirst for participation, and a confidence that excellence is a lively possibility.

The fond backward glance just given exaggerates the goodness of the past and, no doubt, the benign imprint of that past on my life and character. Unfortunately, there are negative limits as well as positive. My surrounding culture was emotionally unexpressive, parochial, judgmental toward others, utterly uncompassionate toward those who "deserved" their plight, and defensive about its own smallness and anonymity. The accentuation of small-town American values carries with it a dark side, a disregard for values that necessarily complement them—interdependence, cosmopolitanism, and a sense of ambiguity.

Religion did not suffocate these other sources of identity. Indeed, in many cases it merely sanctified those small-town American values. But in other cases it reminded us of a larger world, of higher values, and of divine purposes that certainly transcended our lives in that time and place. Above all, it placed the world in which we dwelled into an ultimate context that gave meaning and sacrality to all of it—the good, the bad, and the indifferent. The Christian faith provided the canopy of meaning that responded clearly to the fundamental questions of life: Who am I? What is going on? What should I do?

OTHER STORIES

The contemporary context for growing up is quite different for most. The five great trends spoken of in chapter 1 have far greater impact on young persons than they had on me. Young persons are bombarded with many versions of the meaning of life and the values that accompany those versions. Their peer cultures—often self-consciously adversarial toward the adult, conventional world—exercise much more influence over them. Historical tragedies and ominous possibilities are magnified by mass media. Cultural relativism is the assumed backdrop of modern life. Liberation from inherited constraints promises the exciting realization of the self.

So, life is more confusing for the contemporary young. It would be a mistake, however, to suggest that the formation of earlier generations just simply "stuck." Indeed, the universities and colleges I have been associated with are staffed with many persons brought up under the same general conditions as I, but who have now "fallen away."

For many, the rigid confinement of religious communities was just too much. Sometimes the confinement took the form of a harsh moralism. Many former Catholics saw the taut teachings on contraception, abortion, divorce, and the role of women as too oppressive for them. Such teachings ruled them or loved ones out of the Christian community too quickly. Others found the spiritual and moral discipline of the church loveless—a negation of their being. Many Protestants from conservative traditions reacted similarly.

For most of those who have fallen away, however, the greatest offense was intellectual; while they grew in intellectual sophistication in secular fields and in their general approach to life, the church continued to feed them an eighth-grade articulation of the faith. Too great a gap opened up between their early formation and their intellectual development. This gap was exacerbated by the rampant reductionism in most secular disciplines which ruled out in principle any serious consideration of the religious factor.

Meanwhile, the church withheld from its developing laity the more sophisticated interpretations of its intellectuals. Theological and biblical inquiries which can clear away some of the superficial stumbling blocks for educated laity were not boldly and systematically offered to them at crucial points in their intellectual development. One simply need not accept all biblical materials as literal and scientifically true. Nor does one have to accept every jot and tittle of doctrine as the direct revelation of God. It is not that simple, and the church knows it. Christian faith includes the ambiguities of personal doubt and uncertainty, as well as consciousness of the fragility of all human formulations of belief and practice. We are saved by the graciousness of God in Christ, not by our theological and/or moral rectitude.

Some of those "fallen away" do return. Under the pressure of life's challenges and tragedies, or nagged by a deep feeling of emptiness of life without a transcendent dimension, they return to the church to see if the Christian faith can make mature sense. Others, who have been lightly "inoculated" by a watered-down version of the faith, are prompted to look seriously for the first time at Christian claims.

A RETURN AT DEPTH

Even those such as I who have never physically departed from the church reappropriate the faith in ways that do more justice to the depths and the heights of life as well as the profundities of the faith itself. As life unfolds, persons and events provide us with experiences that cry out for interpretation. When these fuller experiences of life interact with the framework of the Christian faith, one reappropriates Christian meaning at a deeper level. One begins to know what the great tradition has meant by finitude, sin, and grace.

Finitude means that we are limited in our creatureliness. As we move through life we become increasingly aware of the rapidity of that movement. We rush headlong to our ends—to our finish. I seem to have known in their lifetimes a good portion of those now buried in my hometown cemetery. My own life is decidedly past the mid-way point, even given the assumption that no fatal accidents or diseases are around the corner. The body slows down and one needs more orderliness in one's life style. Options that were once plentiful in one's younger days are now drastically fewer. The need to make every effort and every day count increases. The years ahead are surprisingly few.

Besides this consciousness of the fleetingness of time, one has a heightened awareness of how dependent one is. Health, while under some intentional control, is basically beyond our manipulation. We are dependent on deep-running organic processes that are impervious to our understanding and control. Further, we live our lives on the thin ice of patterns of human support that are indeed fragile. Every trip on a highway entails a risk. Economic life is unpredictable. Nuclear catastrophe is a possibility. A spouse may die. Friendships may end. Children may encounter accidents or personal disintegration. Institutions upon which we are dependent may collapse. Fragility is the name of the game; we are dependent creatures.

Finitude means limits on what we can accomplish. We can only love a few people, and oftentimes poorly at that. Surplus energy beyond our strict duties is shockingly low. Necessities of life seem to suck up our time and energy. We are buffeted this way and that by too many claims to handle adequately. Much of what we are able to do seems flawed and half-hearted. The meaning of our work evaporates like a bubble on a stream. We get confused about what we should do with our lives.

These elements of our finitude are made painfully present to us by our capacities for self-transcendence. We look upon ourselves and observe our mortality, our radical dependencies, and our limits. Sometimes this causes us to retreat from life, to escape from our capacities as free creatures into trivial pursuits, restless quests for pleasure, excessive drinking or drugs. Our finitude overwhelms us and we try to escape.

But we cannot. The greatness of our being as free creatures before God will not go away. We continue to be obsessed with ourselves. We become the centers of the world. The world is simply an extension of us. We cannot love God or neighbor because we are caught up in our own struggle for meaning and significance.

Rather than retreat from life, many of us try to become "winners" or attach ourselves to winners in the face of the frailties of our finitude. We defy that finitude by proudly claiming importance for ourselves and our deeds, for our families, schools, companies, professions, nations, or race. In our own minds we elevate ourselves in some way above the common herd so that we can proclaim our significance before God and humankind. Often this leads us to neglect or abuse others in our struggle for self-importance. Human relations are contaminated and eroded. This profound sickness—this obsession with self—is what the Christian tradition has meant by the word "sin." It points to the deep separation we experience, separation from the Ground of our being, from our real selves, and from others. This return to Christian insights in our maturity corroborates their accuracy.

True enough, before our fellows we appear reasonably considerate, successful, self-confident, and "in charge." The conscience-stricken Christian may not appear as a failure. But that assessment is only on the horizontal level in relation to our peers. Before our own internal court and certainly before God's we know that truth about ourselves. Our condition is terminal. There is no health in us. Striving to free

ourselves from our condition leads us into a confusing maze. Efforts
to find some pure and undefiled center of our being only uncovers
more self-obsession, turning ever inward upon itself.

The fact that experience brings us fully into the consciousness of
our sin is not bad, however. It is only when we know the true depths
of our own situation that we will fall on our knees in supplication
to God. Then we will understand Søren Kierkegaard's puzzling remark that it is a comforting thought that before God we are always
wrong.

Thus, a fuller appropriation of our finitude and sin can be the
occasion for a fuller appropriation of God's grace. Indeed, a mature
assessment of one's sin makes *necessary* a reliance upon God's grace.

Above all, appropriation of God's grace means a confidence in
God's saving Word and Work in Jesus Christ. It means faith that God
has retrieved us lost and disobedient creatures through the tender
mercies offered in Christ. Christ has assured us of our significance
and forgiveness. His work has paid the price exacted by our disobedience. He has defeated our foes—sin and death. He has become our
righteous representative before God even as he has represented God
to us. Through our faith we have been engrafted into his death and
resurrection. We are justified by the grace of God in Christ through
faith.

No matter how many ways we might try to articulate the meaning
of God's rescue mission in Christ, we still merely grope for adequacy.
But, nevertheless, the fruit of God's redeeming grace is ours. Instead
of continued obsession with our own mortality, significance, worth,
and achievement, we can relax. The work of salvation has been done
for us. We need only accept in trust what God has said and done for
us. Our strivings are not necessary; in fact, they are an impediment.
Simply accept the fact that you are forgiven, accepted, and affirmed
by God on account of Christ. Nothing more is demanded. God's
salvation is given to us; we are radically receptive.

The crucial identity of ourselves before God is thus established.
We may not look or even act all that differently from those around
us, but internally we know that we are liberated by God's grace in
Christ from the bondage of sin and death. As Luther said, "We are
free Lords of all, subject to none," because we are no longer depen-

dent for our salvation on anything but God's free and limitless grace. Our being is thus affirmed radically by the Author of all things. God has sought us—even as disobedient and insignificant as we are; and we are his. We are special, not because we are intrinsically worthy, but because God loves us.

The personal reception of God's grace also opens the eyes of faith to the liberating moments of grace given to us humans in the midst of our lives that come without religious tags on them. Trust emerges, reconciliation occurs, new beginning is given, and affirmation is received by persons in the nitty-gritty of their lives, whether or not they are Christian. Indeed, in our confused and dark world such events of grace are often not recognized as the gifts of God they are. They are attributed to human agents alone or to luck. Good dramas, novels, and films often portray such events of grace but they rarely name the ultimate source of such events. Christians are simply the ones who recognize the source and give proper thanks and praise to that source: God.

This joyful confidence in God's special redeeming grace does not do away with the ambiguities of life. There are still great absurdities and tragedies. Struggles with family, work, and citizenship continue. Even our belief and behavior may not be on an ever-upward trajectory. But our greatest comfort is that we are not saved by our clear knowledge of good and evil, by our full understanding of God's ways with the world, by our unswerving obedience, or even by our unwavering belief. No, we are saved by God's grace, something much more dependable than our dubious capacities. God's grace affirms us even in our unbelief.

Certainly, this acceptance of God's grace in Christ does have powerful effects on our outlook and behavior, though our status before God is not finally dependent on those effects. First, our outlook on life is powerfully conditioned by our appropriation of God's special grace in Christ. The givenness of our created existence—what theologians sometimes call "common grace"—takes on a new character. In spite of the mess we have made of the creation, the constancy of God in maintaining it and in engaging in ever-new creation is recognized and celebrated. Just as the accounts of creation came after the experience of Israel's redemption in its liberation from Egypt, so a new and vivified appreciation of creation follows the Christian appropriation of God's special grace in Christ.

The beauty and intricacy of life in all its varied forms, the gift of our families, the enriching activities of our lives, the presence of friends, the glorious traditions of excellence in learning and the arts, the opportunities for broadening and deepening our experience, and the persisting allures of nature are embraced with praise and thanksgiving. These gifts common to all humans are hallowed in the eyes of those who have seen the heart of God in Jesus Christ. They come from a Giver whose grace is beyond our understanding. Even though we know that the creation has been distorted by human sin and our lives are therefore fraught with ambiguity, we trust that behind and beyond it all is One who is radically for us.

Further, the trusting reception of God's grace in Christ conditions our will to do God's work in the world. The One who has loved the repentant sinner is beloved by that same sinner. Loving God simply means a fuller intention to do God's bidding. We will fail in our intentions to be obedient because sin is never fully overcome in us, but nevertheless we strive. Each day we are driven back to the grace of God to forgive our failures and to recharge our devotion to God's will.

One often thinks that the main elements of one's identity are freely chosen. We think mistakenly that we "make" our own lives. But as we reflect upon them carefully we realize more clearly how things happen to us. Persons appear "uninvited" to challenge or change us. The cultures into which we are born condition our outlook decisively. Our families firmly shape our character which then in many ways becomes our destiny. World-historical events set the stage upon which our lives are lived. Great religions dominate our world view. Doubtless there is a modicum of freedom that transcends such powerful conditioning, but it can only work within our dependencies, not escape them altogether.

Through these historical, social, and practical vessels we are called and blessed. The Spirit of God works to bring our experience of life and Christian meaning together. We are Spirit-led to hear God's call and do his will.

BIBLIOGRAPHY

For reflections on God and false gods:
Niebuhr, H. Richard. *Radical Monotheism in Western Culture* (esp. "Faith in Gods and in God," 114–26). New York: Harper & Brothers, 1960.

On the search for God in human religious quests:
Eliade, Mircea. *The Sacred and the Profane: The Nature of Religion.* New York: Harcourt, Brace & World, 1968.

On God's dealings with Israel:
Wright, G. E., and R. H. Fuller. *The Book of the Acts of God: An Introduction to the Bible.* Garden City, N.Y.: Doubleday & Co., 1957.

On the human predicament:
Niebuhr, Reinhold. *The Nature and Destiny of Man: A Christian Interpretation.* New York: Charles Scribner's Sons, 1941.

On Christ, revelation, and salvation:
Braaten, Carl. *Principles of Lutheran Theology* (esp. the chaps. on Christology and Soteriology). Philadelphia: Fortress Press, 1983.
Luther, Martin. "The Freedom of the Christian." In *Martin Luther: Selections from His Writings,* edited by John Dillenberger. Garden City, N.Y.: Doubleday Anchor Books, 1961.
Niebuhr, H. Richard. *The Meaning of Revelation.* New York: Macmillan Co., 1967.
Tillich, Paul. *The New Being.* New York: Charles Scribner's Sons, 1955.

On the church:
Ahlstrom, Sidney. *A Religious History of the American People.* New Haven: Yale University Press, 1972.
Marty, Martin. *Pilgrims in Their Own Land.* New York: Penguin Books, 1985.
———. *A Short History of Christianity.* Philadelphia: Fortress Press, 1980.
Walker, Williston. *A History of the Christian Church.* 3d rev. ed. New York: Macmillan Co.; Edinburgh: T. & T. Clark, 1970.

On the church, narrative, and character:
Hauerwas, Stanley. *The Peaceable Kingdom: A Primer in Christian Ethics.* Notre Dame, Ind.: University of Notre Dame Press, 1983.

On growing up in America:
Benne, Robert, and Philip Hefner. *Defining America: A Christian Critique of the American Dream.* Philadelphia: Fortress Press, 1974.

On sin as separation and denial of death:

Becker, Ernest. *The Denial of Death.* New York: Free Press, 1973.

Kierkegaard, Søren. *The Concept of Dread.* Princeton: Princeton University Press, 1957.

Tillich, Paul. *Systematic Theology.* 3 vols. Chicago: University of Chicago Press, 1957; 1973–76.

On justification by grace:

Rupp, Gordon. *The Righteousness of God: Luther Studies.* London: Hodder & Stoughton, 1953.

Tillich, Paul. "You Are Accepted." In *The Shaking of the Foundations.* New York: Charles Scribner's Sons, 1948; London: SCM Press, 1949.

Watson, Philip. *Let God Be God: An Interpretation of the Theology of Martin Luther.* Philadelphia: Muhlenberg Press, 1947; 1st paperback ed., Philadelphia: Fortress Press, 1970.

3

Christian Nurture

You are fellow citizens with the saints and members of the household of God, built upon the foundation of the apostles and prophets, Christ Jesus himself being the cornerstone, in whom the whole structure is joined together and grows into a holy temple in the Lord; in whom you also are built into it for a dwelling place of God in the Spirit.

(Ephesians 2:19–22)

There seems to be a trinitarian structure to human existence. Certainly the theological tradition from Augustine through Luther to H. Richard Niebuhr has argued that. There is a center of value that persons trust and give their loyalty to even as that center reciprocally gives meaning and significance to those who trust it. That center is the power or reality to which the human heart is fastened. It is, as we argued earlier, the "god" of that person. In most instances there is more than one "god." As Niebuhr argued, natural human existence is polytheistic.

The center may be the family, sophisticated pleasure, the nation, power, or as seems so popular these days, "wellness." Usually it is a combination of these centers. At any rate, there is always a "word" of knowledge, advice, exhortation, and affirmation that allows the person to live in relation to the center of powerful value that has been selected for trust and loyalty.

If the center is sophisticated pleasure, for example, a number of "words" are available to enable the pleasure-seeker to live in a deeper relation to pleasure. For those low on the ladder *Playboy* is such a "word." As one moves up, the slick magazines put out by and for each major city give additional aid. *Vanity Fair* and *Gentlemen's Quarterly* are further "words" for the high achievers. Such "words" enable one to live in a sophisticated way before pleasure.

Besides the powerful "god" to which one is related through the enablement of a "word," there is a third dimension of our natural religious life—an ethos, a way of life. The "word" will direct one to the way one *should* live before the center of powerful value. In the case of sophisticated pleasure, the way of life has many different elements. One must eat the right foods and dine in the right restaurants, live in the right neighborhood in the right kind of house, dress in the latest fashions, go to the most chic nightspots, vacation in the "in" places, listen to the right music on the proper stereophonic equipment, and experience sex in the most avant-garde way.

Consistent devotion to such a way of life will of course bring the follower into conflict with other "gods" and their attendant "words" and ways of life. Sophisticated pleasure will exist in great tension with family life, true patriotism, or the quest for power.

In my account thus far I have argued that the God of Abraham—the Source and End of all—is the center of value to which we should give our trust and loyalty. That God, beyond being yet moving in and through it, is also the orderer and sustainer of all things. And because we have disobeyed and fled him, God is also our judge.

In the midst of darkness and chaos, though, God has sought us out; he has called us. God has spoken to us through the "words" of Moses, kings, prophets, and finally, most decisively, and in a radically new way, in Jesus as our Christ. That decisive Word has liberated us to live before that final reality, God.

God, the Source and End of all, has called us to be his people through Christ. God has reached out and claimed us. We have been given our peculiar identity as his beloved. We have been justified by God's grace on account of Christ. Christians are those who have responded to this call. They receive God's blessing with trust and joy.

But Christian existence is not merely passive. God the Holy Spirit enables Christians to forge a way of life—an ethos—that flows out of the Word before that final reality which they trust and adore. Put another way, the Power in which we live is given meaning in Christ the Word, and in the ethos of the Christian community that power and meaning come together. The character and direction of the ultimate power—God—is disclosed and realized in Christ, and that powerful goodness is reflected in the Christian way of life. Father, Son, and Holy Spirit provide the trinitarian structure of the Christian vision.

Christians are called to live according to this relationship to God in Christ. They invite the Holy Spirit to move *in* them and *through* them to approximate the powerful goodness of God in Christ. In this chapter we will focus on the movement of God the Spirit *in* us, nurturing us and filling our cup of being.

This focus on God the Spirit *in* us follows from two considerations. First, there is an intrinsic dimension to our focus. We must attend to our growth and nurture so that we might more closely approximate our nature as creatures formed in the image of God and our status as forgiven sinners on account of Christ. Attending to our growth and nurture opens us to the Spirit's forming us into who we are and wish to become. We are called to live up to our relation to God for its own sake. We wish to "dwell in the house of the Lord," where "goodness and mercy shall follow" us all the days of our lives.

But this focus on the Spirit of God filling our cup of being also has a second dimension, an instrumental one. God the Spirit moves in us to strengthen us for our responsibilities in the world. The filled cup is meant to be spilled, or its contents become stagnant. Strengths are cultivated to be used toward God's intentions in the world. Indeed, our being cannot be separated from our doing. Our enacted responsibilities shape our being. The depth and height of our being before God cannot be fully grasped unless we engage in responsible life in the world. Nor can virtue be forged without having it tested in action.

The major part of the book will be devoted to responsible life in the world. It is important to emphasize here that the Spirit of God that moves *in* us also moves *through* us to others. Nevertheless, unless our Christian being is replenished we will have little to give in service. Our cups of being must have something in them to share. Thus we must attend to Christian nurture.

An additional point must be made before we move to the discussion proper. The disciplined and intentional nurture I will propose is not really a constitutive part of our salvation. Our salvation is a gift of grace to which we are completely receptive. We are saints because we believe in the promises of God in Christ, not because of the holiness of our lives. Rather, Christian nurture is practice at being a trusting son or daughter of our God who already loves us unconditionally as sons and daughters. That love is already assured us from God's side and that is sufficient for our redemption. We need not earn our sainthood. As a *response* to that love, however, we must practice what it means to be beloved of God. We must allow the Spirit to move in us and through us.

PARTICIPATION IN THE
BODY OF CHRIST

We are social and historical creatures, far more than we in our self-obsessed state would like to admit. We are shaped and conditioned by others even though we may not be simply the sum total of those effects. As those kinds of creatures we need to allow the bearer of the Christian story—the church—to "imprint" us deeply. The Christian story must be solidly ingrained in us if the Spirit is to fill us and use us.

In order to rehearse, reinforce, and receive our identity before God, we must hear the stories of God. We must listen. The church insists that the Scriptures be read aloud. It is an excellent practice to follow the readings for the day in the Bible or in printed bulletins. The words can be dwelt upon and savored. In the Scriptures we hear the most direct testimony to God's mighty acts available.

In the church we hear the Word of God preached, not as well as we need it, but nevertheless preachers carry on. In an ideal church, there should be clear interpretations of the Scripture for the assembled body. The objective Word of God should mesh with our own subjective experience. God's call in both Law and Gospel should be directed into the contours of our own lives as twentieth-century Christians. The story must be both told and applied.

We can also hear the music and texts of Christian composers sung and played. In some churches it is possible to hear very high quality renditions of traditional and contemporary music of the church. For many Christians a fine performance of a work such as Bach's "Jesu, Joy of Man's Desiring" can mean an ecstatic encounter with divine transcendence. Most churches must be content with lesser quality but with perhaps just as much, if not more, motivation. Christians can accept those more modest offerings with pleasure and gratitude.

Other kinds of receiving are ours in the sacraments of the church. There we encounter God's Word in action. In Baptism we are received into God's forgiving love even before we can respond. We are gathered into Christ's death and resurrection. We are claimed as God's own.

In the Lord's Supper the forgiving and living presence of Jesus is imparted to us in, with, and under the forms of bread and wine. The palpable and visible signs of Christ's presence are received. Indeed, in both sacraments the Christian finds the cup of being replenished through the working of the Spirit. Our cups run over as the divine presence fills us.

The church's worship also includes active response and participation. We engage in intercessory prayer, sing psalms and hymns, and participate in the liturgies of the church. All these lift up the religious affections of praise, repentance, joy in forgiveness, compassion, moral direction, and hope that are responses to God's initiative. We are trained in religious affections through the churchly teachings and poetry that is ensconced in prayers, liturgies, and hymns.

Further, there are important opportunities in the church for study. An increasing number of churches offer first-class religious studies in adult forums and classes. Laity have stepped forward in eagerness to assimilate a grown-up version of Christian education. Sadly enough, the education of the young has suffered even as adult education has been enhanced. Fewer children come to Sunday school, fewer good teachers are available, and fewer disciplined programs of instruction are mounted. If the churches are serious about nurturing their young in a world as confused as ours, much stronger education will have to be developed. Sunday school, weekday study, confirmation, and youth groups need to be strengthened if we are to "hold" our young.

There is much to say for the fuller retrieval of "liturgical worship" on the part of many Protestant churches, not the least of which are the Lutherans. As these churches have striven to become more "catholic," that is, more inclusive of the whole history and wide scope of Christian tradition, they have grown in their appreciation of the church year, the commemoration of important figures in Christian history, the frequent celebration of the Eucharist, the use of liturgical vestments, the participation of laity in the leading of the service, and the use of worship practices that stretch back to the church's founding. This "liturgical renewal" has contributed strongly to the nurture of Christians. It has strengthened their connection with the saints of God in all times and places. It has heightened the sense of sacred time and sacred space in contrast to secular notions of time as duration and space as undifferentiated area and it has elicited a more varied and richer set of religious affections than the more aural Protestant services of the past.

Two other recent movements have also contributed much to the nurture of Christians. The women's movement and the movement for lay ministry have both encouraged more equality, confidence, and sense of belonging to all members of the body of Christ. While male dominance and clericalism have not denigrated the status of women or lay people before God, these attitudes have tended to make both groups second-class citizens in the church, and this has impeded Christian growth and leadership among these large groups.

Pastoral care is the final element of the church's life that needs to be mentioned. Everyone at some time or another experiences crises in their own lives or in the lives of those near to them. In many cases one is left shocked, depressed, and sometimes helpless. Here it is that Christian love and care are most appropriate. The pastor must see to it that such care goes on within the body, but he or she in no sense is the only one capable or willing to give care. And it is in receiving such care that one experiences Christian love; in giving it one practices and learns the love of neighbor. Both giving and receiving nurture Christian being.

There are many other dimensions of the life of the church—particularly those involving service—that will be addressed later. Here we have focused on those that directly strengthen Christian identity and being. Participation in the life of the church nurtures the quality of one's being before God. We are imprinted with the signs of our relation to God. We taste transcendence and experience how it affects our spiritual and moral lives. We live the story. We become more transparent to the Spirit of God that moves in us.

CHRISTIAN PRIVATE DEVOTION

In addition to participation in the church as a public body, Christian nurture includes private devotion. Personal prayer is a good place to begin. Evening prayers of praise for the day of blessings and morning prayers of gratitude for a safe night are a good place to start. Add to them prayers of intercession for others and of supplication for oneself and one has the beginning of a personal discipline.

Private study is another important ingredient. Daily reading of the Bible, of devotional material specially published for that purpose, or of works of a more explicitly theological nature are all good ways of strengthening one's spiritual life. A lay friend of mine reads the nontechnical work of Helmut Thielicke, the German theologian. Others read the "devotional" work of Dietrich Bonhoeffer, Pierre Teilhard de Chardin, or Henri Nouwen. I enjoy working through Dag Hammarskjöld's *Markings* or Martin Luther's *Day by Day We Magnify Thee,* a compilation of sermons organized for use every day of the church's year.

Some Christians keep diaries in which they reflect on their day's experience from a religious point of view. There is a very good instinct in that habit. It is a very enriching practice to engage periodically in thorough *interpretation* of one's life from a Christian point of view. It is often only in retrospective reflection that we see the hand of God in our life's story. When we are in the heat of the battles of daily life we frequently can discern no pattern in events. But some time later the shape of events becomes clearer. Moments of challenge, of grace, and of new beginning are discernible. Little things—a word from a friend, a painful obstacle, an unforeseen intervention—become occasions for basic changes in life's direction. What we thought we *chose* looks more and more like it *happened* to us. Interpretation can connect all these "moments" into an intelligible story in which God is the writer, we the characters. It is helpful to check these interpretations out with Christian friends (pastors included). This not only holds one's interpretations accountable to others' Christian scrutiny, but it is nourishing for both parties.

One of the major sources of spiritual uplift is great music. When the classical masters express the struggles and triumphs of the human soul in their compositions, we are often touched by the ineffable. Mahler's *Resurrection Symphony,* Beethoven's Ninth, Mozart's piano concertos, or Bach's cantatas bring encounters with transcendence. The objects of the composers' aspirations and the quality of their aspiring lift their music far above what is available at the popular level. Even when this music is not about specifically "religious" subjects, it is transparent to something beyond our mundane existence. Those composers are truly Christian friends who fill our cups until they run over.

There are many other kinds of private devotion that have not been mentioned. Christians have their own patterns. Each effort is a way to open the path for the Spirit to strengthen one's formation in Christ. Then when the challenges of life come—of which there are many—one will have resources upon which to draw.

PERSONAL RELATIONS

Some time ago I wrote a letter to the wife of a childhood schoolmate who had died in an accident. I saw the death notice in my hometown newspaper which came several weeks late. Though I was a bit concerned that my condolences would come at an inappropriate time (too late), I still wanted to express them to her in her bereavement. I ended the letter with wishes for her Christian comfort and hope.

A week after I sent the letter I received a marvelous response. Not only was she pleased to get my letter, but she described briefly their life together, emphasizing their recent renewal in Christian faith and life. While the shock and sorrow were certainly present in her letter, there was a strong affirmation of her husband's life as a gift of God and of hope for his eternal destiny. She ended by asking me for some information about our family's life.

In such an exchange a great deal of mutual support was carried on. I felt buoyed in my own Christian identity by her letter and I suspect she felt the same. And that was only a letter. Far more important in sustaining us are the mutual consolations of Christian friends in person.

Generally, I find that the most supportive persons in my life are neither exclusively members of my own local church nor secular people. Rather, they are a collection of Christian people from here and there who naturally come together. Often there is no "checking out" of denominational membership or even explicit talk about religious matters, but there is a discernible sense of affinity one to another. The comfortable conversation and tacit affirmation then lead to more explicit attention to the delights and struggles of being Christian in the modern world.

Then there are close friends of long standing or companions in a common cause whose edifying presence is indispensable for both support and accountability. They are the ones to whom one goes with troubles or quandaries and from whom one receives advice and solace. Good friends will also hold one accountable to one's own better nature and one's own commitments. A Christian must know how to receive such a ministry to friends and to give it.

Finally, for many Christians the most important giver of support is the immediate family. In the family the day-to-day, close-at-hand affirmation of spouse, parents, children, or siblings is the richest and most steadfast source of human care. They are primary ways that God sustains and blesses us. It is extremely important to cultivate and appreciate these interdependencies. We will have more to say about the family later on.

Personal relations—whether Christian or not, whether placed on a "religious" basis or not—are a key way in which our being is nurtured. In them we are enriched by the interdependencies built by God into the creation. We partially realize our being as creatures of God. Certainly part of this realization is the capacity to enjoy both the personal relations themselves and the activities for which persons come together. In other words, we have fun together. Playing together, engaging in festivities, and celebrating accomplishments are the rich gifts of God as much as more serious and purposive activities.

Moreover, in these personal encounters we are provided models of what it means to be Christian and human. (Unfortunately, we are also provided models of what it does not mean.) As we take the role of those close to us we learn who we are. Both nurturing and modeling also prepare us for our responsibilities in life. They enable us to be and to do.

CULTIVATION OF ONE'S OWN PERSON

Just as with the foregoing general discussion of Christian nurture, attention to cultivation of the self is a bit dangerous. Some might object that this is close to an exercise in narcissism, that is, there is obsessive concern with the spiritual health of the self. Others might say that the chronology is wrong: one is nurtured only in one's active involvement in the world. Act obediently and your cup shall be filled.

There is a certain element of truth in these objections. One cannot focus *solely* on Christian nurture without it becoming cloying and myopic. One's being and identity is obviously shaped by one's doing. Nevertheless, there is a sense in which we must receive identity and strength before we can act with resolve and integrity. Our being precedes our doing.

Furthermore, there is a sense in which we cultivate our own selves—with their capacities for thought, self-transcendence, aesthetic enjoyment, and play—simply because we have been given them as gifts by our Creator. We are not called to refuse them or neglect them, at least not in normal times. There may be occasions when much of this cultivation must go by the board for the sake of some great overwhelming cause, but even then one must attend to the sources of Christian identity and strength.

In normal times we do have the opportunity to cultivate our created selves as gifts of God. We can start with the care of our bodies. The body is a marvelous thing. Its intricate processes are most clearly evident to us only when they break down. Then we realize how dependent we are on their proper functioning for carrying on our daily life and work. The older we become the more we are aware of that dependency.

Therefore, to respect our bodies as the wonderful gifts of God they are we must care for them. Increasingly that means scrutiny of what and how much we eat. Our society is becoming much more knowledgeable about the foods that are good for us and those that are not. Without being slavish or obsessed about proper diet, Christians respect their bodies by sensible eating and drinking. It goes without saying that persistent abuses of them through immoderate drinking, eating, or smoking are a violation of the stewardship of our bodies. Further, such abuses tend to deflect us from becoming the kind of persons we aim at.

Bodies are also meant to be used and enjoyed. An aesthetic joy accompanies the excellent action of the body. To have body, mind, and spirit cooperating fully in an activity like running, tennis, or golf can be likened to a sacramental experience. The body's expression becomes transparent to the grandness of God's gift. As the runner in *Chariots of Fire* put it: "When I run I can feel his pleasure."

Those moments are only occasional, however. Most of the time the use and enjoyment of our bodies are more mundane. Sometimes the exercise of our bodies is sheer duty. But whether joyous expression or stolid duty or some more likely mixture in between, that exercise keeps them in a shape appropriate to their gift status as well as in proper condition for use in the responsibilities of our active lives.

The cultivation of the mind and spirit is also a Christian duty to the self. Our capacities for rationality and self-transcendence are at least part of what makes us "a little less than the angels." Thus, we ought to exercise them as fully as capacity and opportunity allow. Knowledge of human history, the natural world, the arts, politics, world affairs, and the work of the human imagination in novels are appropriate results of the exercise of human reason and spirit. Such knowledge helps us transcend the narrow borders of our own small worlds. Combined with virtues such as empathy and imagination, knowledge of a world wider in both time and space than our own aids us in the critical appreciation of the proper ends of our own lives as well as our society's. We are often enabled to recognize the tawdriness and perversions of current social trends and make the proper corrections in our own lives. In short, there are Christian grounds for cultivating the self toward the ends at which a liberal-arts education aims. "Christian humanism" celebrates all the exercises of the mind and soul that are true, honest, just, pure, lovely, and good.

Third, cultivation of the self includes those activities that are recreative—hobbies, leisure activities, and vacations. Many of the activities we discussed under cultivation of the body and mind already fall in this category. The true mark of recreative activity, though, is its capacity to help people relax and "get away from it all." Gardening, stamp collecting, travel, fishing, watching TV, enjoying a cabin on a lake, walking in parks are examples of the hundreds of things people do for simple relaxation. And they are necessary for everyone, but especially for those whose work is full of strain or pressure.

Let us conclude this chapter on Christian nurture by recapitulating its main points. Our trinitarian faith involves a trust and loyalty to God made possible by the reconciling work of Jesus Christ. Furthermore, Christian faith entails a way of life that is shaped by the Holy

Spirit. The Holy Spirit moves *in* us, filling our cup of being, and *through* us as we spill that cup on behalf of others. This chapter has focused on the nurturing of Christian life by the Spirit. Our Christian being is nourished by active participation in the church, by personal devotion, by Christian fellowship, and by the cultivation of our own person. All these activities open Christian persons to the work of the Spirit *in* us. The Spirit uses them.

That work, however, cannot be dissociated from the Spirit's push toward service to others. Only when the cup is emptied will it be filled by the Spirit with new and fresh wine. Engagement in the world is like breathing out; without it one cannot breathe in. But the reverse is also true.

This movement of the Spirit *through* us in obedient love for others is given concreteness in our particular responsibilities in the world. It is also conditioned by that very concreteness, so that obedient love takes on surprising shapes at times. It is to those places of responsibility that we now turn.

BIBLIOGRAPHY

For additional study on the Trinity:

Sayers, Dorothy. *The Mind of the Maker.* New York: Harcourt, Brace & Co., 1942.

Tillich, Paul. *Systematic Theology.* 3 vols. Chicago: University of Chicago Press, 1957; 1973–76.

On the Holy Spirit:

Lampe, C. W. H. *God as Spirit.* New York and London: Oxford University Press, 1971.

Ramsey, Michael. *Holy Spirit.* London: SPCK, 1977.

On worship:

Moule, C. F. D. *Worship in the New Testament.* Richmond: John Knox Press, 1962.

Underhill, Evelyn. *Worship.* New York: Harper & Brothers, 1937; reprinted, Westport, Conn.: Hyperion Press, 1983.

On personal devotion:

Bonhoeffer, Dietrich. *Letters and Papers from Prison.* London: SCM Press, 1971; enlarged ed., New York: Macmillan Co., 1972.

Hammarskjöld, Dag. *Markings.* New York: Alfred A. Knopf, 1964.

Luther, Martin. *Day by Day We Magnify Thee.* Philadelphia: Fortress Press, 1982.

Lutheran Book of Worship. Minneapolis: Augsburg, 1978.

Nouwen, Henri. *Compassion.* London: Darton, Longman & Todd, 1983.

————. *The Living Reminder: Service and Prayer in Memory of Jesus Christ.* New York: Seabury Press, 1977; reprinted, New York: Harper & Row, 1981.

————. *Making All Things New: An Invitation to Life in the Spirit.* New York: Harper & Row, 1981.

PART
II

THE CALLING OF
THE CHRISTIAN

As each has received a gift, employ it for one another, as good stewards
of God's varied grace: whoever speaks, as one who utters oracles of God;
whoever renders service, as one who renders it by the strength which
God supplies; in order that in everything God may be glorified through
Jesus Christ.

(1 Peter 4:10–11)

If, in the midst of our age-old confusion and rebellion, we are
called by God to be his own through his grace in Jesus Christ, we are
also called by that same God to service in and to the world. The Spirit
that works *in* us to nurture our relation to God also works *through* us
to strengthen our relation of service to the world. The cup of being
that is filled at the table of the Lord is meant to be spilled in the Lord's
errand into the world. Blessed by God's free grace in Christ we are
called to be a blessing to others. Luther caught the connection well.
We are simultaneously, he said, "Free Lords of all, subject to none,
and servants of all, subject to all."

The call of God and the calling of the Christian are not meant only
for priests and pastors, exemplaries and heroes. Every ordinary
Christian has been sought out by God's Word. Likewise, every Christian is called to responsible service in the world. We do not have to
look far for the locations of our service to one another. Those locations are very close-at-hand. They are also very ordinary—family,
work, state, and church.

The following three chapters will examine the calling of the Christian in general. We will look at the characteristics of our places of responsibility, the various stages of moral development, and the distinctive features of the Christian's sense of calling. Part 3 will focus more particularly on each place or sector of our calling. It will aim at more specific guidance for Christian life in the world.

4

Places of Responsibility

Our initial theological assumption here is that God has not left the ordinary day-to-day world bereft of his presence. God's special grace in Christ does not mean the withdrawal of the common grace of God that sustains the world. We are not plucked by that redeeming grace from a God-abandoned world. On the contrary, we receive God's grace by our faith which then becomes active in God's struggle to maintain and develop the world.

In, with, and under all the forms of responsible life on earth is God's sustaining power. The structures of family, state, economy, church, and education are grounded finally in God's preserving and directing will. Some theologians have called these structures the "orders of creation," others the "orders of preservation."

These structures are viewed as the effects of God's dynamic law of creation. God's energies hold all forms of human life into being and direct them toward "covenantal" existence. God's governing power gives moral order to our common lives. Prompted by his undergirding law, our lives are gathered into responsible relations with others.

A useful image to convey this law of covenantal existence is the magnetic field. God's intentions are like a magnetic field. If we order our lives to conform to the patterned currents of God's intentions we live in harmony and peace. If we live in opposition to them we are caught up in conflict and chaos. We bump into and injure others as well as ourselves. God's dynamic law is a gift that in the long run brings blessing if obeyed, pain and suffering if rejected. In the short run there are no simple correlations between virtue and blessing.

One does not have to search for these forms of responsible life. They are given with the territory of life and are impossible to avoid. I am a member of my parents' family, connected to them and to my brother and sister. I am the husband of my wife, father of four children. I am a teacher at a church-related college. I am a citizen of the city of Salem, the state of Virginia, the United States of America, and the world. I am a member of College Lutheran Church, the Virginia Synod, the Evangelical Lutheran Church in America, and the Lutheran World Federation. I belong to many voluntary associations, in a number of which I have official responsibilities. I have circles of friends that gather about each of the above responsibilities to whom I have at least implicit commitments. Each of these places of responsibility can open out to ever-broader communities, straining toward the fully inclusive covenant that God has with his Creation. But they can also contract into narrower circles of interest and concern about which we shall say more later.

Let us now be more specific about the characteristics of these places of responsibility. What are the marks that accrue to my roles as a family member, a citizen, and a worker? What are the characteristics of the guises God uses to maintain and order the Creation? There are at least three major characteristics worth discussing at length. These places of responsibility and the roles associated with them are *sanctioned, dynamic,* and *ambiguous.*

SANCTIONED

Every society has certain purposes it needs to have fulfilled if it is to exist in a reasonably healthy and orderly way. Families need to have children and nurture them. Economies need to produce wealth by coordinating the productive energies of the people. Schools need to educate the young to become critical recipients of their cultural heritage, to become effective citizens, and to be productive workers. Governments need to defend their societies, maintain order, and pursue justice.

In assuring that those purposes are pursued effectively, societies develop a system of "oughts" and "ought nots," "musts" and "must nots" around these purposes. Those directives are enforced by an arrangement of rewards and punishments. It is important that the directives "stick." For instance, a citizen must pay her or his allotted portion of income tax. The IRS applies rules that punish those who do not remit their proper taxes.

These societal sanctions first of all aim at shoring up certain nonmoral, technical "excellences" that are indispensable for the workings of a particular activity. A manager in a business must know and be able to perform the proper roles of the manager. The student must know how to study properly. The parent must know how to run a household. The government figure must know the levers of power and be able to use them.

These technical "excellences" have moral dimensions but cannot be reduced to moral capacities. These are worldly practices that simply must be mastered in order for the social order to work. The church has no particular expertise in them nor does it have a blueprint stipulating their exact shape. These "excellences" have an integrity of their own that cannot be replaced by good moral intentions. Luther recognized this when he announced in typical robust style that he would rather be governed by a wise Turk than a foolish Christian.

A society cannot be content with mere technical excellence, however. These worldly capacities can be used for the wrong purposes or in the wrong way. Military skills can be employed by terrorists as well as by legitimate armies. Thus, there is a moral guidance system that attempts to stipulate the proper ends of the capacity as well as the proper way it is to be employed. Medical skills generally cannot be employed to kill people nor can they be used without the consent of the recipient. At least those are moral presumptions. Without a good share of agreed-upon moral presumptions within a society, any number of dazzling technical excellences will not suffice. The society will descend into a chaos made more violent by the technical proficiencies it has attained.

Sanctions, therefore, deal with both moral and nonmoral capacities as they aim at encouraging and guiding the actions that sustain a society. We can identify at least three levels at which sanctions operate: the external level of law and culture; the internal level of conscience; and the deepest or most transcendent level of divine intentionality.

EXTERNAL—LAW AND CULTURE

The most obvious sanctions in a society are its laws. They stipulate the minimum behavior prescribed or proscribed by the society. While laws are certainly not the same as morality—which is much more expansive—they are the distilled minima of the society's moral consensus. Laws proscribe certain behaviors (murder or robbery) and prescribe basic levels of responsibility (family support or registration of eighteen-year-olds for military service). They cannot enforce more than a minimum without becoming ineffective nor can they deal directly and immediately with the internal motivations for action, though there is evidence that in the long run they affect moral attitudes. For instance, it is doubtless true that laws against racial discrimination have influenced the attitudes of Americans toward fairer treatment of racial minorities. Conversely, a relaxation of law can affect moral attitudes—witness the easier moral acceptance of abortion occasioned by permissive abortion laws.

Theologically viewed, the positive laws of a society are restraints against its most overt evildoers. They provide a dike of protection that is crucial for basic social order and security. They also provide positive direction for the commonweal. They are instruments of God for social preservation insofar as they roughly measure up to the standards of God's justice.

At the same time laws are dependent on and nourished by something less tangible than written codes. That is the system of normative values, practices, and meanings that make up the culture of any given society. Culture is embodied in mores, conventions, expectations, and habits. In England, for example, all these conspire to ensure that people "queue up" (line up) while waiting for a bus or for service in a store. At a more serious level, culture dictates that a set of parents care for their children. Patterns of social approval or disapproval strongly sanction responsible parental behavior. A punishment worse than prison is visited upon those hapless parents who are caught abusing their children and then show up on the front pages of newspapers, pictures and all.

These cultural sanctions operate in all areas of life. Though less uniform and less firmly held than earlier, they continue to shape our society in ways that maintain a basic social and moral order. In places where the cultural system has broken down badly, social and moral chaos make life utterly miserable. Only the strongest individuals and communities are able to survive in such circumstances, and then under great stress. We can all appreciate the great resilience of many black families who survive and thrive in the most impoverished and disorganized ghettoes of our large cities.

Most of the time, however, the cultural system runs more intactly; we take for granted this glue that holds together our normal everyday lives. The highly refined patterns of social practice are what give each culture its particular character and flavor. Thus, the guidance systems are certainly not only negative but also constructive, providing the very stuff of our common life in society.

We should not forget, however, that there are "iron teeth" in these patterns. They provide sanctions for what societies consider necessary and proper. It should be added that every institution within the broader society has its own normative patterns. A business organization has very specific expectations of its participants, often stipulating even how they should dress. These expectations are carried by institutions over time, frequently embodied by exemplary figures, traditional practices, and favorite narratives. Thus, every person is caught up in a number of normative cultural systems surrounding their places of responsibility. These are objective—out there.

INTERNAL—CONSCIENCE

Every person also internalizes to some degree the external characteristics of the surrounding cultures. What is external becomes internal. The person builds up a "social self" by taking the role of significant other persons who are present to that person. Naturally, there are many of these "significant others" so that the "social self" of each person is complex and varied. The complexity of social formation ensures that each person is different from another. But there is usually a common enough base in the surrounding culture to provide each person with a fairly specific sense of right and wrong, proper and improper, good and bad. Society's guidance system thus becomes internalized.

Specific communities within the broader society are sometimes more powerful than others in the moral socialization of the self. Deeply religious families often shape their children with very clear

notions of moral behavior. Churches reinforce and build on those
notions. They can be at sharp variance with those of the broader
society and thus set up conflicts within those children when they
become older. Mennonite young people, for example, must decide
which path they are to follow, that of their elders in the faith or that
of the "world."

It would be a mistake to suggest that we are simply the sum total
of all these social environments. While they indeed condition us
heavily, they do not completely determine us. There is a center of
self-conscious freedom within the self that creatively shapes the
various social "inputs" that it meets. That freedom also responds to
an inner structure of the self that presses toward fitting relations with
itself and others. The structure of the essential self, sometimes called
"original justice" by theologians or "moral reason" by philosophers,
provides a further court of adjudication within the self. So, the internal life of the moral agent is a lively and complex one. While powerfully conditioned by its own social history, it also has access to more
universal moral structures that must be related dynamically to that
history by the spontaneous center of the self, the "I." The internal
constitution of the conscience is therefore a delicate and lively process, never completely predictable. It is also buffeted by the centripetal
forces of human sin which prompt it toward self-centeredness. Moral
virtues such as courage and resolve aid in the self's struggle with sin
as it meets the challenges of life. Further, the experience of that
struggle in the journey of life can strengthen and enrich the conscience.

DIVINE

The external and internal sanctions we have discussed so far have
been handled primarily in a sociological and philosophical way. The
exposition is more indebted to George Herbert Mead than the Bible.
Even so it is not unbiblical, for the Bible reminds us that we are not
atomized individuals but part of ongoing historical communities. The
difference in our present situation is that our social formation is more
complex than in biblical times. Where there was once one religious-
political-economic-social unit there are now many distinct and
sometimes divergent spheres of social formation. Young persons are

often more shaped by the expectations of their peer group than by their parents or the church, for instance.

This situation makes the final level of sanction even more difficult. The final level pertains to God's will for our covenantal existence. How do the divine intentions relate to the patterns of our lives in state, society, economy, church, and family? These spheres may and often do tug in different directions. Which come closer to God's will than others? Which are so far out of kilter that we have to resist them? Which are worthy of Christian obedience?

At this point we cannot engage in a substantive discussion of *what* God's intentions in these various spheres might be. We can only reflect briefly about *how* we might make up our minds about them. That process is primarily one of discernment on the part of the church and Christian individuals. Christians in community and individually must discern for their time and place what God's purposes are in these places of responsibility. There is no avoidance of this ongoing task.

Discernment is first of all a task of the community of faith. As we have emphasized above, persons are decisively shaped by their social history. Christians are unlikely to be Christian without the powerful ongoing conditioning of the church. The church, however, does not engage in its task in an arbitrary manner. It must first take the Scriptures seriously, for it is there that the most direct witness to God's revelation is recorded. God's purposes in both Law and Gospel are revealed. The fundamental lineaments of God's will are proclaimed.

It is well known, though, that the Bible can be made to support almost any opinion if it is subjected to selective ransacking. Thus the Scriptures are complemented by traditions of interpretation. The living community of the faithful, responding to the Word of God in the Bible and at the same time relating it to the challenges of its day and place, makes continuing efforts to discern God's will in the world. The ongoing reflection of the church—of theologians, bishops, pastors, and laity—is the medium through which the Holy Spirit enables us anew to discern God's intentions for us.

For example, the church has determined that the practice of racism—embodied in the American past in legal segregation and in the present in the South African system of apartheid—is clearly at odds with God's intentions for covenantal existence in both church and society. While there is ample room for disagreement on how apartheid should be dealt with, there is Christian clarity on its basic immorality.

Though discernment is fundamentally a task of the church community, there is also an individual dimension to it. For one thing, the church may be wrong and Christian individuals may need to hold the Lord's will over against the church itself. Luther, for example, criticized and then reformed many of the practices of the Roman Catholic Church of the sixteenth century because he discerned that they were out of line with both the Bible and the best of the Catholic tradition. For another, the church cannot possibly assess every particular situation in which the individual lives. When it tries to become that specific, it becomes ridiculous, if not oppressive.

Therefore, each Christian, taking serious account of the church's teaching, must discern the correspondence of social practice in each place of responsibility with God's own will. Of one thing the Christian can be sure: the practice involved with every place of responsibility falls short of a full approximation of God's will. But it is also likely that those practices have *some* affinity with God's intentions or they would fall into disarray. For it is a Christian conviction that the legal, cultural, and internal levels of social sanctioning cannot in the long run diverge radically from their ground in God's will. The Lord's purposes will not, in the long run, be ignored or perverted with impunity.

Christians have an additional level of concern than do their secular counterparts. Besides conforming to the external and internal sanctions of their places of responsibility, they in addition want to make sure that those sanctions and their relationship to them are moving in broad consonance with God's will, not against it.

In this way Christians acknowledge that their lives in their places of responsibility are held accountable to purposes that transcend their broader culture and the more limited institutions in which they live their lives. There is an authoritative will beyond this world that stands in both judgment and affirmation of it. Christians cannot simply accept the demands of their places of responsibility without submitting them to the scrutiny of a higher authority—God's will as it is perceived through the discernment of the Christian community.

DYNAMIC

The second major characteristic of the roles associated with our places of responsibility is that they are dynamic—they change. In recent history they seem to be involved in accelerating change. Take the roles of wife and husband in a marriage, for example. Even in our present generation these roles have been subjected to enormous changes. A couple now are often concerned with two careers instead of one. This has meant a revision of how and where a couple live, how they engage in parenting, how family finances are controlled, how participation in church and other voluntary associations is allotted, and even how partners name themselves and their children.

We can give many other examples of dynamic change. We no longer think of ourselves necessarily as having only one career. Large numbers of persons change careers at least once. Parenthood has changed rapidly as other institutions and subcultures—the school, the youth subculture, television—compete vigorously for the attention of the young. Family and church must struggle mightily for the loyalty of the children. Citizenship has become increasingly complex as American responsibilities have widened and become more ambiguous in recent decades. The post-World War II consensus has eroded and that fact has challenged U.S. citizens with unexpectedly difficult choices which do not fall into comfortable black-and-white categories. As the church has become more aware of its own diversity on a worldwide scale, it has faced challenges concerning the basic nature of its identity and mission. Voices of the Third World within the church have both tested and enriched our church involvements.

These mighty changes are the results of the engines of social change we mentioned in chapter 1—technological change based on applied science, increased knowledge of our cultural relativity, the spirit of liberation, secularization, and a revolution in rising expectations. While we can manage and sometimes resist these powerful forces, there is no escape from their relentless pressures. Only a cataclysm of the first order would bring them to a halt.

Therefore, we are caught up in persisting change. This means a constant redefinition of our roles in our places of responsibility. Even when we resist change we redefine ourselves in relation to an environment that is changing. The couple that insists on a traditional-style marriage and family life become more aware of their choices in a changing and challenging environment. They are also viewed differently by those that follow the new trends and therefore they take on a new self-image in the midst of their traditional practice.

In this dynamic whirl we learn as Christians from two things. We learn from the practice of our religious and moral traditions what values we want to preserve no matter what. Fidelity within monogamous marriage is a nonnegotiable ideal. We also learn from our experience of the changing world. God's energies toward emancipatory changes as well as human creativity and sin are involved in these great currents. Christians communally and individually must travel through this uncertain journey with a critical eye, discerning which of their values must not be changed, which can and ought to be reshaped in order to live on in new ways, and which of them lead to resistance to what is going on in the world.

Being caught up in dynamic change also teaches us about our finitude. The large societal changes affect us in our places of responsibility. Business persons, for example, must increasingly face international competition in an ever-widening world market. Their own responsibilities are expanded and made more complex by forces beyond their control. Dynamic changes impress upon us our fragilities. Moreover there is change built right into our own beings regardless of what happens in our environment. We pass through the whole cycle of life whether we wish it or not. Each stage means changes in self-definition. Passing from full-time work to retirement means a challenging struggle for a new identity for many persons.

Thus, the dynamism that permeates all our places of responsibility makes our lives a real adventure with appropriate elements of exhilaration, terror, and uncertainty. God holds the history of us puny creatures in God's hand. Christians have the lively task of keeping the faith in the midst of the journey.

AMBIGUOUS

The final major characteristic of the roles involved in our places of responsibility is their ambiguity. In fact, the institutions wherein these roles are enacted, the roles themselves, and our activities within them are all shot through with ambiguity. Human life enacted in families, the economy, the state, the voluntary sector, and the church is characterized by a volatile admixture of good and evil. Paradoxically, the capacity for evil grows alongside the capacity for good. Only things with a genuine allure of goodness—family life, for example—can be tempting enough to be objects of idolatry. Pure goodness or pure evil are therefore difficult to find in the locations of our common life. We are much more likely to find a beguiling ambiguity.

The first thing we must affirm about these structures of our common life is their goodness. They are the good vehicles of God's creative care for the world. They are instruments of God's common grace. They order and support our lives. Anyone who experiences the warm mutuality of family life, the intrinsic rewards of productive work, the exercise of civic duties, the participation in a lively community of worship, and the joys of the friendships that adhere to each of these sectors knows something of the great gift of life, the providence of God. Our being is sustained in them. They are our daily bread.

We cooperate with the Creator when we take active responsibility in them. Even those who have no religious consciousness attending their involvement in these structures participate in the creative work of God. Through the myriad of coordinated human actions in the world, God gets his creative and preserving work done. We are interwoven into this fantastic system of divine governance. It is the good stuff of our lives.

If this goodness were the only dimension of our existence, our lives would be hunky-dory, but they would not be human. Such a one-dimensionality would ignore our finitude and our sin, both of which are inescapable traits of our human predicament. Our finitude entails that our lives in our places of responsibility are fragile. They are open to the dynamic change we spoke of earlier. Further, they are vulnerable to accident, failure, and conflict. We are smart enough creatures to sense that. What parents are not worried about the dangers that face their children as they grow up? Just the threat of auto accidents is enough to disturb the most serene parent. What children are not concerned about the dangers of disease that can afflict their aging parents?

But our worries are not limited to such external fallibilities. We also worry about our own performance in our roles. Can we meet the requirements of our job, the expectations of our fellow workers, or even more stringent, the demands we place on ourselves? Over and beyond these, can we meet what God requires? These external and internal pressures are sources of deep uncertainty. Added to that is the inchoate sense of our own insignificance and mortality in the whole scheme of things. In moments of reflection we catch glimpses of our own weakness and the impending facts of our own decline and death.

In short, because we are beings capable of self-transcendence we stand outside ourselves and observe our own dependencies, fragilities, and shortcomings. An inevitable concomitant of this self-consciousness is anxiety. Because we are anxious, however, we are also creative. Our sense of incompleteness and fault is a spur to creative energies that drive us into more purposive activity. Without a measure of this anxiety, for instance, the business person would become flat, sinking into complacency. The anxiety arising in a competitive situation, reminding the business person of her or his vulnerability, is a spur to constructive action. In addition, that person is anxious to use her or his gifts to their full extent in order to satisfy a self-imposed demand.

At the same time, however, anxiety is also the occasion for sin. Anxiety occasions sin on both the individual and corporate level. Individually, the anxiety that issues from our self-transcendence becomes the occasion for passivity, sensuality, or pride. All these three are manifestations of a fundamental self-obsession that ensues when we cannot accept our mortality, insignificance, and fault. Because we cannot trust God and his grace, we mistakenly and sinfully make ourselves the center of ultimate concern.

Those whose fundamental posture is passive are thoroughly convinced of their insignificance and fault. At root the problem of passivity is a religious problem. The person is not able or willing to accept the affirming grace of God. The result is a loss of confidence, self-worth, and hope. There is a serious depression of the spirit— talents and energies are wasted.

The sensual response to our ontological anxiety is more active. But its activity is aimed at escaping the greatness and responsibility of our lives by immersing itself in pleasure. The sensualist aims at pleasurable negotiations with the environment, seeking out pleasures in food, sex, entertainment, and other creature comforts. If such aims are pursued consistently, the sensualist refuses to take responsibility for roles in the sustaining structures of life. But such a life is not a happy one, for pleasure cannot satisfy the deeper longings for significance and meaning. The search for "kicks" accelerates and a vicious circle ensues—the frenetic search for pleasure leads to increasing emptiness.

While both of these forms of self-absorption tend toward irresponsibility, the third form curiously enhances, but then perverts, responsible life. In this form anxiety is dealt with by asserting the self. The self and its activities are elevated above its surroundings by the sheer force of will. The self inflates itself. This is accompanied by contempt for or neglect of others. But pride leads to an active engagement with the necessary social tasks of life. There is an unstable mix of authentic pride in the capacities of the self and an inauthentic pride prompted by an underlying insecurity. This amalgam drives the self forward with ambiguous effect.

We are all infected with combinations of these forms of sin. That inevitable condition is what the classical theological tradition has called "original sin." It is an inescapable bias of human life. This bias, especially in the form of pride, is injected into social life and institutions.

While individuals have the rational capacities for self-criticism and the spiritual capacities for repentance, institutions have much less. Thus, human collective life has a powerful tendency toward narrow self-interest. The restless pride of individuals filters into collective life in ways that make collective life more dangerous than individual. That danger is compounded by the greater power accruing to groups.

Groups, then, have an inclination toward closure, or what H. Richard Niebuhr called the "ethics of defense." They defend their self-interest more assiduously and project their assertive wills more vigorously than individuals. This is most certainly true of large collectives like the nation-state or multinational businesses. But it is likewise true of smaller groups.

Our pleasant neighborhood in Virginia, which still contains a working farm, was recently "threatened" by a plan to erect a senior-citizens' home on one of the choice sites of the farm. As it happened the site was tucked into one of the remote corners of the farm, out of view of the neighborhood. It should be mentioned that our locale is made up of friendly Christians of a most helpful sort. But when the plan for the home was announced, it was as if the heavens were falling. The nicest people engaged in vigorous organizing to keep the home out and they were successful.

This kind of defensive exertion of collective will is unfortunately characteristic of all institutional life, to a greater or lesser degree. Everything from the family to the nation-state is infected by this social sin. There are no innocent individuals or groups.

Therefore, our lives in our places of responsibility are inescapably ambiguous. The family is a major object of human idolatry. Businesses exert their power as much as they can. Churches claim to be the true church. Large nations dominate or neglect small ones. Moreover, our roles within these human groups are pressured by the same tendency toward closure. I claim too much for myself in family life to the detriment of my wife and children. I see my role and the role of our department in our college as more important than they are. And so on. Conversely, institutions make undue claims upon the persons who take responsible roles. Nations claim the lives of young persons in their violent struggles with other nations. Businesses demand total loyalty from executives, forcing them into an idolatrous existence. The dynamics of sin set up conflict, chaos, and death. Evil is painfully present in our fallen world.

The obviousness of evil leads some Christians to see the structures of our common life as totally under the dominion of death. For them the only proper response is resistance. But our perspective here is different. The institutional forms in which we take on responsible roles are both the gifts of God's ordering and creative providence *and* the arena of sinful human pretension. Sometimes these structures bend in a wholly demonic direction. Christians must discern this and resist. But most of the time our social institutions are ambiguous. Often we are fortunate to live in circumstances that are ambiguously *positive*. Then Christians are called to enrich and extend those positive qualities. Even when they are ambiguously negative, the Christian calling is to make improvements where that is possible.

It is a miracle—a wondrous gift of God's common grace—that the whole interlocking system of social institutions that make up our society sustain and order life as well as they do. For this we give thanks. But the whole system is unstable and ambiguous because human freedom is used for both good and evil. Christians cannot rest complacently with either the system or their roles within it. They are called to be the critical leaven that leavens the lump. In order for them to become that they must develop into mature Christian moral agents. We turn now to the topic of moral development.

BIBLIOGRAPHY

On the orders of creation, law, and the governance of God:

Forell, George. *Faith Active in Love.* Minneapolis: Augsburg, 1954.

Gustafson, James. *Ethics from a Theocentric Perspective.* Vol. 1, *Theology and Ethics.* Chicago: University of Chicago Press, 1981.

Wingren, Gustaf. *Creation and Law.* Philadelphia: Muhlenberg Press; London: Oliver & Boyd, 1961.

On the sanctions of culture:

Berger, Peter. *Invitation to Sociology: A Humanistic Perspective.* Harmondsworth: Penguin Books, 1963.

On the social self and conscience:

Meade, George H. *Mind, Self and Society.* Chicago: University of Chicago Press, 1924.

Miller, Donald E. *The Wing-Footed Wanderer: Conscience and Transcendence.* Nashville: Abingdon Press, 1977.

Nelson, James B. *Moral Nexus: Ethics of Christian Identity and Community.* Philadelphia: Westminster Press, 1971.

Pfuetze, Paul. *The Social Self.* New York: Bookman Associates, 1954.

On the contribution of the Bible to moral discernment:

Ogletree, Thomas. *The Use of the Bible in Christian Ethics.* Philadelphia: Fortress Press, 1983.

On the ambiguity of roles in places of responsibility:

Niebuhr, H. Richard. *The Responsible Self.* New York: Harper & Row, 1978.

On the nature of individual and social sin:

Niebuhr, Reinhold. *Moral Man and Immoral Society: A Study in Ethics and Politics.* New York: Charles Scribner's Sons, 1932.

———. *The Nature and Destiny of Man: A Christian Interpretation.* New York: Charles Scribner's Sons, 1941.

5

Moral Development

When we were trying to lease our house for a sabbatical year some time ago, we came across two applicants. The first, an up-and-coming English scientist, was recommended by a neighbor. After an interview with him, we signed a simple lease that stipulated our respective responsibilities. Even before the family arrived, a nearby house came up for sale. Immediately upon arrival the scientist began hunting for a sublease candidate for our house because he wanted to purchase, not rent.

Subleasing was not discussed in our agreement though we made it clear upon his inquiry that we certainly did not want other occupants in our house without our assessment of them, and that was impossible since we had already left. Nevertheless, he told us he would proceed with subleasing since that was not prohibited in our written agreement. He obviously wanted to buy the house that was for sale and was going to do that whether we liked it or not.

As luck would have it, a second applicant who did not know the house was already leased wrote us. He was a philosopher teaching at a church-related college. But the most significant characteristic of the family was their Christian Reformed affiliation. That small denomination is of Dutch origin and noted for its strict religious and moral discipline. After a telephone conversation, we released the Englishman from our prior agreement and leased the house to the Christian

Reformed family, sight unseen. We rested easily during our sabbatical with no further problems concerning our home. It was in great shape at our return.

That little story illustrates the difference in moral "styles" assumed by persons. We recognized qualities of moral character in the second family that we thought were absent in the first. We were pleased to entrust our home to the second but very reluctant to do so with the first, after their respective characters were revealed.

This chapter aims at understanding the various stages of moral development, among both persons who claim Christian identity and those who do not. Moral development, unlike the appropriation of God's grace in Christ, is not only the prerogative of Christians. Indeed, non-Christians often put Christians to shame when it comes to moral seriousness.

Moral development corresponds to the four levels of sanctions that were discussed in chapter 4. Egoism, the lowest level of development (which can scarcely be called "moral") corresponds with the most overt kind of sanction—the coercion of law and convention. External obedience is demanded of the egoist by the external pressures of law and convention. The actions of the egoist are disciplined insofar as these pressures are effective.

Heteronomy, in which loyalty to the group rather than the self is paramount, corresponds primarily with cultural expectation and custom. In this case, however, those expectations are internalized and become a genuine source of moral guidance. They stipulate the quality of relations among persons in the group. Persons are loyal to a larger world than themselves.

Autonomy corresponds to the inner pressures of the essential structure of the self—to what theologians call "original justice" or philosophers "moral reason." The autonomous moral agent legislates and sanctions his or her own moral action, not in the sense of inventing an original moral guidance system but in the sense of creatively shaping what has been socially given in dynamic relation with the internal call of the essential self. This autonomous moral stage has the potential of being more open and creative than the heteronomous stage.

Theonomy, wherein the agent aims at becoming a vehicle of God's intentions through the Holy Spirit, corresponds to the divine level of sanction. The moral agent intends to become transparent to a reality and will beyond itself—the divine reality and will. Sanctification replaces sanctioning. The energies of the Holy Spirit gather up human moral capacities and shape them toward God's intentions.

The discussion of theonomy will be postponed to chapter 6 since it is synonymous with a full-blown expression of the Christian's calling. We want at this point to focus on the first three stages of moral development as they are expressed in our concrete places of responsibility.

Before we begin our analysis of egoism, heteronomy, and autonomy, several important qualifications are in order. First, it is important to emphasize that these moral stages are not simply self-generated by the moral agent. The characteristics accruing to each are shaped by others—the family, the community, the church, and the broader culture. We do not just decide to be autonomous or heteronomous. The movement from one stage to the next is prompted by interactions with those who are our "significant others." Certainly the Christian Reformed family did not just decide to be respectful of property, clean, and honest. They were shaped by their religious tradition mediated through family and church. No doubt they would see the Holy Spirit working through all those agencies. The fact that they are strongly conditioned by their history does not mean that their own moral agency is denied. They assented to that history and chose it for their own. Further, their own creative appropriation of it involved some revision and change. Nevertheless, their communities played a decisive role in their own moral character.

Second, it is also clear that these stages are not hermetically sealed compartments through which one progressively moves, step by step. They really are only meant to be provisional categories that shed some light on our moral situation. We are often in more than one at the same time; we are mixtures of the characteristics of several. Moreover, while there is "progress" in the move from egoism through heteronomy to autonomy, that "progress" is open to increasing peril. The autonomous person can claim more self-sufficiency than the heteronomous and thus be more prone to arrogance and pride. Finally, there can be regress as well as progress. In a challenging situation egoist tendencies can often emerge as the real substance of the character of the moral agent, rather than the higher qualities that provided an attractive façade.

Third, it should be reiterated that these characteristics of moral development cannot be substituted for the nonmoral excellences appropriate to each place of responsibility. Moral autonomy on the part of a student cannot take the place of intelligence, discipline, and a clear set of educational goals. Both nonmoral and moral virtues are indispensable elements in the responsible student, just as they are for other persons of responsibility.

EGOISM

Egoism commends the self's enhancement as the main principle of direction. Whatever it is that the self wants is pursued. In its purest form it promotes unheeding, narrow self-aggrandizement. It uses all the self's rational capacities to manipulate persons or situations for the benefit of the self. Egoism is selfishness.

Egoism rarely appears in its pure form, however. There are at least two reasons for this. The first is that the self rarely has the unrestricted power to exercise its selfishness. There are few Caligulas in history; Friedrich Nietszche's Superman exists only in the imagination. Most humans, even the most powerful, are rational enough to recognize that they are limited by other persons and groups beyond their control. Therefore, they must play their cards wisely, deferring to others when it is to their advantage but dominating or ignoring others when they must and can.

Thus, most egoism has a prudential side to it. Only sociopaths adapt a bull-in-a-china-shop egoism. Most forms are far more sophisticated and therefore more dangerous because they are more disguised. So, most egoists do not appear as conniving cads. They often obey laws and conventions because it is to their advantage to do so. They pursue their self-aggrandizement in slick ways. To do otherwise would be disadvantageous.

My prospective lessee of some years ago did not appear as an unscrupulous fellow. It was to his advantage to make a good impression on me, and he did. Moreover, before he undertook to sublease our house in violation of the spirit of our agreement he made sure

I had no legal recourse to force him to stay in our home. Seeing none, he proceeded to pursue his interest in spite of our objections.

There is a second reason why the stridency of pure egoism is mitigated. That has to do with the fundamental structure of our being, which presses us toward mutual relations with others. It also has to do with healthy cultural influences that encourage moral sensitivity. While it is clear that we are always buffeted by the contrary tuggings of a divided self, it is also true that our sinful tendencies rarely suffocate our moral sense completely. There is a war in our members that neither side wins decisively. That is an anguishing element in our human condition.

But that element means that even the egoist usually maintains human connections where affection and loyalty qualify the drive to self-aggrandizement. There is often some small bit of commitment to a larger entity than the self. There is honor even among thieves. Without those connections the self would wither into isolated madness, for the self cannot forever deny its fundamental structure. Thus, most egoism is mixed with enough counterflow at least to provoke a bad conscience.

Our broader culture reflects this inner war of the dividend self. There are all kinds of communities—both large and small—that encourage and practice moral commitments to entities larger than the self. Currently, though, there seem to be just as many influences encouraging the aggrandizement of the imperial self.

In its grossest form, popular authors advise persons to "look out for number one," to "win by intimidation," and to "get rich quick." Advertising, reflecting popular attitudes, exhorts people to "grab their gusto while they can," to "turn it loose tonight," and to "have it all." At least some forms of rock music commend immediate kicks through sex, drugs, and violence.

More sophisticated endorsements of egoism abound. Some sexual and feminist liberation movements support a self-centeredness that discourages any commitments that could entail sacrifice or pain. Business philosophies indebted to Machiavellianism or social Darwinism legitimate the self-aggrandizing drive. Interestingly enough though, each of those philosophies dampen pure egoism by suggesting that selfish actions will be transmuted to a larger good by some automatic mechanism, be that natural selection or some invisible harmony. Such machinations are the compliment that vice pays to virtue.

The effects of such cultural inducements have already been discussed. Confusion, the erosion of marital and familial bonds, and a declining sense of civility are all evident. While the sphere of private life is difficult to regulate by law, legal remedies proliferate in public life to manage the chaotic, centrifugal forces set loose by part of our culture's endorsement of egoism. Public liberty is diminished by necessary controls on persons and groups who no longer govern themselves in a trustworthy way.

In such a situation it is the threat and effectiveness of external sanctions that are crucial. For human sin leads to rapacity if not checked. Therefore, theological ethics has generally endorsed coercive measures to maintain a minimal moral order. God uses the coercive force of law as a dike against sin. It would be a mistake to think that a society could be sustained only by such means, however. It would gradually descend into social chaos or oppressive tyranny if it had only the resources of egoism upon which to rely. Egoism must be contained by forms of social cohesion that go beyond it.

It would also be an error to think that egoism is present primarily in the obvious sinners among us. On the contrary, all humans, even the best and the brightest, are afflicted with a bias toward selfishness. The Christian tradition has pointed to the incurvature of the will. Instead of opening outward toward God and the neighbor, the will turns in upon itself. This condition plagues every human being.

Indeed, it is sadly true that religion itself is easily infected by egoism. The selfish desire for heaven and avoidance of hell, so prominent in much of the Christian tradition, is too often the real motivation for participation in Christian religious life. Take away those external sanctions and a good deal of observance disappears. It has been argued that one of the reasons for the waning of Christian religious participation in the West has to do precisely with the loss of belief in such external sanctions.

Even if we are not motivated by such religious impulses we are still not free of the basic selfishness that distorts our essential selves. Those who think they are free of selfish motives may be the most dangerous egoists of all. Straightforward egoists may at least possess the virtue of lucidity about their motives. They may also be the most predictable in the consistent cynicism of their viewpoint. But let us not praise vice in any way; there is already too much support for it in contemporary culture.

HETERONOMY

We move now from the basically amoral approach of egoism to a distinctly moral one. If morality has to do with the quality of voluntary and mutual relations among persons, then heteronomy is a giant step forward. In egoism the principle of motion is the self's enhancement. In heteronomy the principle is loyalty to the social unit to which one belongs. Heteronomy literally means a "different" or "other" law. One is directed not by whatever the self desires but by what society expects. H. Richard Niebuhr used the image of "man the citizen" to describe this approach. Persons assent to the norms of the group to which they belong and order their moral lives in harmony with its expectations.

A negative appellation given to this approach is "other-directed." But certainly heteronomy need not be so viewed. If we agree that to a great extent we are shaped by our social history, then most of the substance of our moral lives comes through its impartation by others. Our Christian Reformed tenants were decisively shaped by their ethnic and religious background. They continued to be loyal to that ethos and we benefited from the virtues instilled by it. Certainly their other-directedness was of high moral quality.

Much depends of course on the societies to which one belongs. We all belong to many, running from worldwide religious communities and the nation-state to local family units. Each has their own set of expectations to which "man the citizen" is answerable. Such a description is not far from how most of us lead our lives. Without these varied communities and the social mutuality they provide our lives would be arid indeed.

"Man the citizen" is characterized by a basic loyalty to his various communities and to their patterns of expectations. A good example of such a person might be an uncle of mine in Nebraska. He has been formed by very distinct communities and his allegiance to them has never been suspect. He is a Nebraska farmer, a member of an extended family, a Lutheran, and a patriotic American. Each of those societies has left an indelible mark on him. In fact, most of his attitudes and behavior patterns are internalized reflections of those societies. For instance, he would never vote for a Democrat since his loyalties are to the conservative anarchism of Nebraska small-town and rural culture. All politicians are suspect from his point of view, but Republicans with their antigovernment rhetoric are the lesser of evils.

Uncle Herman is the salt of the earth though. His particular family and religious culture has formed him toward a gentle kindliness that is its best fruit. The simple and direct expression of his communities' virtues is as admirable as it is predictable.

It would be very misleading to leave the impression that heteronomy is characteristic only of the uneducated and humble. All up and down the ladder of class culture people are "loyal to their own kind." Every profession has its ethos that imprints the attitudes and behavior of its practitioners. There are strong correlations between social groups and the moral convictions of their members.

Some of the most insufferable heteronomy is exhibited by those who think they are free of it. The academic world is composed of many whose "conventional wisdom" is considered by them to be anything but conventional. But their moral, political, and economic opinions are awesomely uniform. Challenges to those opinions from within or outside academe are haughtily dismissed without serious reflection. Each group has its sacred conventions.

One only catches a glimpse of that heteronomy when one breaks with the consensus. Then the weight of group expectations and one's conformity to them become distressingly clear.

Such an awakening to the heteronomy of academic culture occurred for me about six years into my teaching career. At the very early stages of my teaching I saw myself on the "cutting edge" of social, political, and cultural change. I was sharply critical of the "establishment" and the culture of the late 1960s reinforced my opinions. My students and most of my colleagues "ate it up," as the saying goes. In the early seventies, however, I experienced a change in my opinions and began challenging the conventional wisdom of the group. It was then that I saw how uncritical that received wisdom, and my own involvement in it, really was. I saw that for some time I had been enslaved to the expectations of my students. I was getting needed "strokes" from them and this led to an unthinking conform-

ity on my part. I had been part of a heteronomous culture and it took
some doing to get free of it, at least to some extent.

The expectations of our significant others weigh heavily on all of
us. We want and need to belong. It is good to belong. But there are
dangers. One is that loss of critical independence which is important
for both the person and the group. Another is the tendency to get
caught up in and also reinforce the intolerance of strong groups. My
uncle, for example, does not take kindly to persons who do not fit
the profile of his various reference groups. A further problem
emerges when the claims of various groups conflict. The heteronomous person has few independent grounds to adjudicate the con-
flicting claims.

Nevertheless, the larger loyalty, the earnest social solidarity, and
the reliability of "man the citizen" are all worthy of note. Many
serious Christians are in this stage. Of course, one can only say that
when one assumes the generally positive moral quality of the groups'
expectations. But assuming that, it is clear that God uses such communities—and the citizens within them—to sustain and govern
God's creation. God also uses the conflict between them to judge the
pretensions of sinful humanity. The clashes of nations and empires
are the occasion for those heteronomous moralities to be judged.
Heteronomy has its dead ends, just as egoism does.

AUTONOMY

Autonomy is a hotly debated category in current discussions of
morality and our discussion of it will not downplay that fact. On the
one hand, Western philosophical ethics have striven for an autonomous morality—one which flows from some universal base in reason,
intuition, or experience. When philosophers claim to have arrived at
such an approach, as Immanuel Kant thought he had in the nineteenth century, they celebrate that achievement because it frees morality from its bondage to particular communities and establishes a
universal ground accessible to all human beings. There are then independent grounds that can be used as an Archimedean point from
which to affirm or reject the claims of community-based moralities
(heteronomy) and from which to adjudicate conflicts between different moral claims. Western ethics have been characterized by such
a quest for a universal base.

Such an approach need not be antireligious. In fact, most of Christian tradition affirms such a universal base. Saint Paul believed the law of God was written on the hearts of all persons. No one could plead moral ignorance. The Catholic tradition accepts such a universal base in reason; the law of nature can be read by all rational beings. Even Luther affirmed such a rational base for morality. He argued that "civil righteousness"—moral behavior in social affairs—was available to pagans as well as Christians.

It is important for Christians to search for and affirm such a universal morality. Christians believe that there is a structure to the essential self that provides a universal ground, which may appear in human reason, intuition, or experience. God orders his world through the moral actions of all persons, Christian or not. There are moral persons who have never come into contact with Judaism or Christianity.

On the other hand, there are real problems with autonomous ethics and morality. In recent years those problems have been pointed to vigorously by both Christian and philosophical ethicists. For one thing, the charge is made that the real substance of what is proposed as the product of autonomous reason is in fact the moral tradition of the particular cultures in which the proponent is immersed. Kant's categorical imperative—treat others as ends in themselves—sounds very much like the Golden Rule. For another, such trust in a "higher" or "universal" morality tends to blind people to and wean them from the communities where virtue was actually practiced and imparted. "Enlightened" persons are expected to transcend concrete moral traditions. Further, as persons do in fact separate themselves from those organic traditions, their moral guidance systems often become thinner and more minimal. The same thing happens to larger societies. As we argued in chapter 1, the "triumph" of the liberal spirit—which certainly seeks an autonomous morality—has led to a public ethos where the only moral principle seems to be that of free consent.

The fact that autonomous morality attempts to establish itself independent of any particular world view, while a strength, is also a weakness. It separates morality from a larger view of the world which grounds, deepens, motivates, and gives meaning to moral life. Without that richer context, morality is made to survive on the thin gruel of free-standing rational principle.

Nevertheless, in spite of its ambiguity, we place autonomy in a category "above" heteronomy. Autonomy is "inner-directed," not in the way that egoism is, that is, expressive of arbitrary desire. Rather, autonomy means moral self-direction according to critically appropriated moral norms. Those moral norms may come from tradition, reason, or experience. The mark of autonomy is its attempt to justify them on the basis of universal kinds of arguments or evidence. An autonomous person not only has a grasp of *what* is moral, but also *why* it is so.

Such an approach is valuable because it tries to rely on persuading others who may disagree—by appealing to common grounds in reason or experience. The search for those common grounds allows for more open discourse and tolerance than heteronomous morality, which does not search for common ground outside its own perspective.

Autonomous persons also tend to articulate their moral convictions in a broadly intelligible way that is accessible to a variety of persons. They try to distill a universal essence out of the particular traditions that have shaped them. Thus, "treating persons as ends in themselves" becomes a distilled essence of many biblical injunctions.

Because of the quest for a universal ground that transcends particular communities and their practice, autonomous moral agents can be more critically creative than their heteronomous counterparts. In the business world, those who have a critical and creative edge to them are more likely to become leaders than those who cannot go beyond the current expectations and practices of the firm.

One very common expression of autonomy is what one could call "pragmatic utilitarianism." Persons in this camp are committed to increasing the total amount of good in the world. They pursue that goal in experimental ways—testing this or that alternative by trial and error. They are intelligently practical in selecting the means to their general end. They do operate with limits, however. Not everything goes. There are means—often intuitively sensed—that go beyond the pale of moral acceptability.

Many business persons—both Christian and non-Christian—exhibit this orientation. One must admit that they are authentic moral agents. And they operate pretty much out of a secular frame of reference. If religious morality plays a role, it is an indirect one through the early formation of their character and through the continuing nurture of the church. Their on-the-job consciousness remains thoroughly secular.

As people living in a modern, pluralistic, and secular society, we observe many responsible persons of this type. They are genuinely and reliably responsible. In fact, it is sometimes threatening to religious professionals that so many Christian lay persons operate as well as they do in this predominantly autonomous mode.

So, we need not find weakness where there is little. There are enough problems with autonomy without inventing more. We have already mentioned the protests made by Christian ethicists like Stanley Hauerwas and philosophers like Alasdair MacIntyre. Other weaknesses can also be mentioned. First, the flexibility that comes from this more critical approach can easily lapse into confusion. Lack of moral centeredness can be mistaken for tolerance. Conversely, persons who have critically worked through their own moral stance may claim too much in terms of moral knowledge and virtue. Theirs can be a dangerous kind of arrogance in which those who disagree are looked upon with contempt. Autonomy gives too much nod to the well-educated and articulate; it has a rationalistic bias. Finally, autonomy can lead to demands for self-sufficiency: one must do everything oneself. There may be little openness to supportive possibilities in the situation itself. God's presence may not only be ignored but also denied.

Therefore, it is wise to insist on the continuing ambiguity of autonomy. There can be real gains over heteronomy but each gain has an accompanying peril. Nevertheless, it is important to recognize and affirm the presence of this secular version of moral responsibility among persons acting in the world, not least among many Christians.

The living expression of these stages of moral development—along with the expression of nonmoral excellences such as intelligence and discipline—gets the work of the world done in each place of responsibility. God governs through these expressions, whether acknowledged or not. They are the masks through which God rules. There are many sources of moral cohesion and guidance in the Creation that God uses for its preservation. Yet, while we have argued that both the places of responsibility and the moral development of agents within them are grounded in God's governance, there has been little or no mention of a particularly Christian calling within them. It is to the subject of Christian vocation that we now turn.

BIBLIOGRAPHY

On moral development:

Erikson, Erik. *Childhood and Society.* New York: W. W. Norton, 1963; anniv. ed., 1986.

Fowler, James. *Stages of Faith: The Psychology of Human Development and the Quest for Meaning.* New York: Harper & Row, 1981.

Kohlberg, Lawrence, and A. Hewer. *Moral Stages: A Current Formulation and a Response to Critics.* New York: S. Karger, 1983.

Piaget, Jean. *Biology and Knowledge: An Essay on the Relations Between Organic Regulations and Cognitive Processes.* Chicago: University of Chicago Press, 1971.

On criticism of liberalism:

Hauerwas, Stanley. *The Peaceable Kingdom: A Primer in Christian Ethics.* Notre Dame, Ind.: University of Notre Dame Press, 1983.

MacIntyre, Alasdair. *After Virtue: A Study in Moral Theology.* 2d ed. Notre Dame, Ind.: University of Notre Dame Press, 1984.

6

The Christian's Calling—Toward Theonomy

I appeal to you therefore, brethren, by the mercies of God, to present your bodies as a living sacrifice, holy and acceptable to God, which is your spiritual worship. Do not be conformed to this world but be transformed by the renewal of your mind, that you may prove what is the will of God, what is good and acceptable and perfect.

(Romans 12:1–2)

This chapter is the heart of the book. The two chapters spent thus far in part 2 on Christian calling really had very little to do with *Christian* calling. This chapter must make clear the uniqueness of the Christian life by pointing to its vital center.

The two preceding chapters constitute a most important prelude to this one, however. Positively, they have been a way of locating the Christian life in the everyday, common world. That world is replete with institutions such as the family, economy, state, and church in which we take our responsible roles. Those roles are sanctioned, dynamic, and ambiguous. Moreover, those institutions and roles are the means by which God governs and sustains the world. Christians find themselves in them and, except in very unusual circumstances, are called to the Christian life precisely in those places.

In addition, Christians are themselves in various stages of moral development, not at all unlike other persons. Again, God uses the moral energies expressed in each stage, whether or not the persons expressing them are Christian. Christians can and should applaud moves away from egoism toward higher stages no matter who does the moving. So, it does not hurt our case to be worldly, for the world is finally God's. It is the arena for Christian responsibility.

The two preceding chapters are also offered for negative reasons. They characterize human existence under the law, not the gospel. If they are accurate, they should depict an agonizing ambivalence. Life in the world is good, but it is also bad. Responsible life in the family has great benefits, but it also has great risks and terrors. Work gives satisfaction but is accompanied by demands that are always pressing and sometimes staggering. When one takes the whole system of responsibilities seriously it is almost overwhelming.

When one looks inward, the pressure point increases. We erect demanding standards for ourselves and honestly find ourselves wanting. When we assess ourselves according to God's requirements we are even more miserable. Then we invent ploys to hide our misery before God and others. Those lead to self-righteous attempts to justify ourselves before God and others, but that never quite works.

Life under God's demand—his law which operates in all the structures of life—is finally one big accusation. That demand drives us to despair at moments when we are most honest with ourselves, though a good deal of our waking lives is spent trying to prevent those moments from occurring. These moments of dread—which also accompany efforts at moral development that proceed without grace—are not the result of God's intent. They are rather the effect of our separation from God, others, and our essential selves.

Our own lives duplicate the life of the species. Human history became so mired in its own confused disobedience that God initiated a new covenant to retrieve us from our own darkness. Likewise, our contemporary lives under the old covenant—the law—are manifestations of that same confused disobedience, even when we try to obey. Life in the world is fraught with debilitating ambiguity. The sin of the world from the outside and our own sin from the inside conspire to spoil the goodness of God's gifts.

The upshot of all this is that life in the world—even conscientious, responsible life—cannot extract itself by itself from its own sinful predicament and from the accusation that comes with that predicament. We are driven by the very dynamics of life to open ourselves to something beyond ourselves to establish our worth and to provide a sure foundation for our moral vocation. For Christians that "something" is the grace of God in Christ. That liberating grace is the key to Christian existence. It is what gives Christian identity and morality their uniqueness. It is what transforms moral responsibility and development into Christian calling.

The Christian life is the lively response of the Christian to God's justifying grace in Christ. We are brought to God's grace in Christ and nurtured in it by the work of the Holy Spirit. The Spirit works in us to nurture responses of faith, love, and hope. Those very responses are then used by the Spirit working through them to benefit the world. In the following we will delineate the moral meanings of faith, love, and hope as they are expressed in and through the places of responsibility we have been given. As faith, love, and hope do indeed become active in our responsibilities, the actions of the Christian become self-consciously transparent to the deeper intentionality of God in the world. Christian life moves toward theonomy, wherein God's intentions are expressed through the lives of Christians.

It is important at the outset to emphasize that we cannot possess or claim certain development toward theonomy. Even in our best responses we remain both justified and sinner. The reign of the Old Adam within us resides uneasily with the new being given by God's grace in Christ. There may be marked development toward this mode, but there may not. At any rate, God's saving grace is not dependent on such development. We are saved by the grace of God, not by the frail strength of our own faith, love, and hope. It is an authentic mark of Christian piety to exclaim: "I believe! Lord, help my unbelief!" We could add: "I obey! Lord, help my disobedience!"

One of the most difficult issues raised by this strong emphasis on justification by grace through faith on account of Christ concerns the role of our own spiritual development and moral action. If all the work for our redemption has been done for us, if forgiveness and affirmation are offered to the repentant heart unconditionally, if trust in God's grace in Christ is all that is required for salvation, what and why is there anything left to do at all? That is the question put to those who insist on a radical notion of grace. If nothing is dependent on our own work, then why be morally serious?

Such a problem arises, I believe, only if the justifying grace of God is seen as some abstract quality or quantity that can be transferred like money to those who believe. If grace is some discrete entity that can be drawn upon as a person draws upon a bank account, then the question of moral seriousness arises. But if one considers our interaction with God as an intensely personal one, the problem diminishes.

Consider the parable of the Prodigal Son. The main point concerns the graciousness of God to forgive those who earnestly repent of their sins. It is a story of the gospel; it is good news. God is like that. We can trust in God's steadfast grace. God has demanded nothing but repentant return.

But other points can and must be made. First, there is something for the son to be repentant about. He has squandered his inheritance and himself in a sensualist spree. He has violated his relationship with his father by wantonly despising his father's intentions for him. The father's love for the son overcomes the wrath of his judgment upon him without for a minute suggesting that the son's actions were acceptable. The father's mercy did not mean an approval of the son's sins.

The son's response to such mercy would be renewed love for, trust in, and loyalty toward his father. The parable does not say this of course. Its focus is not on the son's further response to his father. But certainly such an extrapolation is not out of order. If he who is separated from his father by his own foolish disobedience is reunited with him solely through the father's gracious forgiveness, the most likely response on the part of the son would be greater love for the father as well as obedience to his will.

Forgiveness and affirmation are objectively offered to repentant sinners on account of Christ. But even repentance cannot arise without spiritual and moral seriousness. It is an effect of our sense that we are bound to God and his will even while we are lost and disobedient. Further, when we are enabled to accept God's gracious offer we are at the same time inevitably drawn to a love for God and his intentions in the world. We cannot authentically accept the grace of God in Christ without spiritual and moral seriousness. Upon receiving forgiveness, the prodigal grew in love for and obedience to his father. Likewise, when we authentically hear and receive the gracious Word of God in Christ we respond with strengthened faith, love, and hope. Only those new strengths are an effect of the grace of God in Christ. We no longer need to obey in order to be saved.

We are obedient because we have been saved. Faith does not free us from obedience, but rather from false notions about the role of obedience.

What then are the effects of God's grace upon our lives in our places of responsibility? What are the fruits of the Holy Spirit as it moves through us? What does theonomy look like, even in its partial and fragmentary realization? The answer is simple and obvious. The Spirit strengthens us in faith, love, and hope. But the real challenge emerges when we must relate those Christian qualities to our lives in the daily world. Then the question becomes: How do they relate to our roles in the places of responsibility?

FAITH

Besides strengthening the posture of faith in relation to God, the Spirit opens the eyes of faith to a *deeper level of meaning in God's world*—the world of everyday responsibilities.

As we argued earlier, each place of responsibility provides a vehicle of God's care for the world. A theonomous mode of existence discerns that. The eyes of faith perceive the presence and action of God in the ordinary.

For example, we can describe our family lives on different levels. On one level we can sketch them in a mundane, matter-of-fact way. For instance, a description of our family might run as follows. Our family of six provides a rich context of mutual responsibilities and affections. I am the primary breadwinner. My wife administers the home. The children are in various stages of development, the eldest already married but the youngest still needing a great deal of parental attention. Basically, we have warm and fulfilling relations and no one among us is "alienated."

A psychologist specializing in family life could rather easily analyze our family on this level. But such a perspective would finally be deficient in understanding the full meaning of our family as seen by the eyes of faith.

There is a deeper level of reality operating that is not accessible to secular social and psychological approaches. Children are seen as mysterious and miraculous gifts of God. They are not simply accidents or even intentional products of our parental decision. They are something more. God was deeply involved in the marvelous processes that brought them forth. They in all their self-conscious particularity were "thrown" into existence to us. We are their stewards for the time they are entrusted to us. They came from the creativity of God's love and they go to an eternal destiny.

We are called to care for them as gifts of God. That means, above all, respect and care for their lives. It means bringing them up in the faith. It means being faithful to the baptismal vows we made at their baptism. It means contributing to their being in every way we can.

This additional level of meaning supplies a seriousness and depth that the mundane, secular frame of reference lacks. The family, as a place of responsibility, becomes transparent to the creative and sustaining energies of God.

Work has a similar dimension. I can look at my job as a college teacher at the superficial level as simply a way to make a living. I have to fulfill certain requirements in order to receive my monthly check. With more effort I can earn promotion and tenure. If I perform the external expectations of my role a certain minimal level of meaning is achieved. But such a meager amount would scarcely sustain me over the long haul of a teaching career.

Another level of meaning may appear at a thoroughly secular level. My work is more than making a living. It is a source of deep satisfaction to me as well as a benefit to the students and the college. Such additional meaning would be capable of sustaining me much better than the earlier instrumental level. Indeed, this level of meaning is the highest available to many persons.

But the eye of faith peers even deeper. My work as a teacher of Christian theology and ethics meshes with the intentions of God to have his revelation known and understood. God uses my teaching in his enlightenment of the world, even though my teaching will obviously not fulfill God's full intentionality. Teaching Christian theology and ethics is a very serious business, having to do, at root, with God's revelation of himself.

Perhaps it is too easy to claim this deeper level of meaning for work that has explicit religious content, as mine does. Other "secular" teaching, the objection might be made, presents a greater difficulty for this sort of interpretation. But that is not true. No matter what the subject matter, as long as it is an authentic field of human learning, teaching is a way that God builds up humanity. Work in manufacturing, business, services, and the home can become transparent to God's care for his creatures and creation. It is true that some work, when it actually harms the creature and creation of God, cannot be interpreted in this way. Drug trafficking, for example, is obviously contrary to God's intentions for humankind. Other endeavors, both decisively negative and ambiguously negative, could be listed. The church and the Christian must judge. In most cases we can see a deeper religious meaning in our work.

Let us not be romantic, however. Some work seems so burdensome or trivial that such interpretations seem far-fetched. In those cases, meaning of the sort we are talking about might be found in family or church life, or in voluntary associational activity. But even so, we should not close off such meaning for those involved in activities that we find distasteful or trivial. I remember a visit to a drop-forge in a farm-implement factory. I thought operating such a forge was the closest thing to working in hell one could imagine. Noise, heat, dirt, and the ever-pounding shock. Upon talking to the men working there, though, I found that they had great affection and pride for their work. They were doing an important, skilled, and difficult job—and they were doing it well.

Such a deeper level of meaning does not imply that all difficulties and ambiguities disappear. They certainly do not. Every kind of work entails its drudgeries as well as its moral ambiguities. But such qualifications do not dispel that deeper level of meaning.

The life of citizenship can be interpreted in a similar way. Beneath the more mundane levels is the challenge to interpret the life of the nation as an arena for divine intentionality. As I exercise my responsibilities as a citizen, I am involved in the larger processes through which the Lord of nations governs the life of nations and the relations among them.

Responsible life in the church can be more obviously transparent to divine intentionality. The church is not only a context of sociability, an instrument of social welfare and action, a school for morals, a repository of sacred music and rites, and a platform for religious speech, though it is all that. At a deeper level it aims at becoming the earthen vessel through which God addresses his Word to the world. When it fails in that task, just as when other human institutions fail in theirs, that deeper level of meaning is diminished and it loses its potency.

There are other places of responsibility where this same mode of interpretation applies—voluntary associations, friendship, recreational activities, and the like. The point is that in each area the eyes of faith sacralize our ordinary existence. What was once mundane and matter-of-fact becomes transparent to something more. This way of looking at things can make all the difference in the world, morally speaking. As I live as family member, worker, and citizen, I am caught up in something much more than the flat, one-dimensional world available to the secular viewpoint. I am caught up in the governance of God. This fact adds a sacrality and holiness to ordinary responsibility that cannot fail to increase moral seriousness. My action is of ultimate significance, not in the sense that it is higher or more important than anyone else's, but that it connects, no matter how imperfectly, with what God is doing in the world.

Thus, the Holy Spirit working in us opens the eyes of faith to deeper dimensions of reality in the ordinary responsibilities of life, even though they are tarnished by our own confusion and sin. That same Spirit also works in us to call us to our particular mission in those places of responsibility. That is, the Spirit moves our faithfulness toward a heightened personal intentionality within the contexts of family, work, and public life. We see the divine activity not only in the world about us, but in our own particular mission in that world.

Put another way, we discern a call or a series of calls. As we have already emphasized, such a call from God comes not only for clergy. Each Christian is called to particular missions in the world. Opening the eyes of faith that we might see our mission, the Spirit lures us away from ambiguity toward unambiguity. We are called to become like a polished arrow in the quiver of the Lord.

The location of this strengthened intentionality is precisely in the places of responsibility we have discussed—family, work, state, and church. We are generally not called to jump out of the common structures of life, although in a small number of cases this might be true. Most likely we are called within those places where God is already doing God's creative and preserving work.

Such a general answer does not help those who wonder about what kind of work they are called to, or what kind of activity as a citizen or a church member ought to be theirs. In response we can only suggest a process of discernment that might be helpful.

The first step in such a process is to reach a certain clarity about ourselves. We need to assess our own gifts, talents, capacities, interests, and satisfactions without illusion. This does not mean we are complacent about all those things, simply accepting who we are at that moment. We know we will grow as we engage our call. But we must begin with a realistic assessment of who we are so that we are oriented to real possibilities, not sentimental dreams. As the parable of the Talents suggests, we are called to use productively what we in fact are given, not what we lack.

A moving example of such clarity was exhibited by the business manager of a school with which I was once associated. Al was an intrinsically lonely and shy man who had trained for ordained ministry but early on discerned, as had the church, that he was not "cut out" for such an intensely social vocation. So he became a business manager for institutions of the church. In that role he became very respected and beloved for his sensitive care for lonely students. He had assessed his own weaknesses and strengths accurately and began to exercise his very weakness (shyness and loneliness) as a means to be of service to others. He could spot a lonely student at one hundred paces. And he helped them in his own quiet and unobtrusive way. His life of service was a model of a certain kind of clarity about himself.

A second step has to do with awareness about our world. There is both a universal and a particular pole to this awareness we are commending. The universal pole augurs for an expansive consciousness about what is going on in the world, particularly where suffering is present. Such an awareness inhibits complacency about one's own security and comfort. There are always serious needs, both near-at-hand and afar. The particular pole means a focusing on those needs that are particularly compelling. One might be that of a friend who needs special attention. In terms of work, it might mean a job that urgently needs doing. Or a cause that powerfully beckons. Christian consciousness cannot float on a stream of universal concern; it must focus on places where needs are especially evident and go to their depths.

These two steps—clarity and awareness—deal with our destiny. God has given us a certain measure of talents and capacities. We have been formed toward specific interests and dispositions by communities that we did not choose. A goodly number of our aptitudes were shaped before we became mature. Likewise, the world in which we live, with all its possibilities and limits, was "given" to us. We had little or nothing to do with its shape. We were "thrown" into our particular time and place.

A third step, the work of our freedom illuminated by the Holy Spirit, discerns our own particular call at the juncture of our capacities and the needs of the world. As Frederick Bueckner has put it: "The place God calls you to is the place where your deep gladness and the world's deep hunger meet." The beckoning call of God exhorts us to gather up our capacities to mesh with God's work in answering the world's needs. A real theonomy emerges at such moments. Our lives become self-consciously transparent to the will of God for us.

One should not think of this call of God in a grandiose way. Few are called to be the movers and shakers of the world. Most of us are called to be loving fathers and mothers, effective workers, solid citizens, and loyal church members in the ordinary places we already know. On the other hand, the "call" can lead to extraordinary achievements in extraordinary places. A Mother Teresa and a Dag Hammarskjöld both felt God's call to pioneering work.

The call of God, though sometimes intensely private and individually received, is more often mediated through the insights, advice, and encouragement of sisters and brothers in the Christian community. Those significant others not only aid in discerning one's particular mission, but they can also be very helpful in holding one accountable after the decision has been made.

Certainly one could not discuss the Christian's particular call without mentioning the role played by spontaneous occasions of "opportunity." History is unpredictable; the unforeseen and unplanned happen. A new person comes "accidentally" into one's life. A job offer comes unexpectedly "out of the blue." A major event changes the course of history, closing off old opportunities but opening up new ones. A tragedy changes one's life trajectory.

As we look at the story of our lives, as much seems to happen to us as we choose. Nevertheless, there are dispositions and capacities that enable one to respond to those opportunities, just as there are objective needs that make those opportunities seem compelling. And there is the delicate breath of the Spirit that brings all these factors into a sense of "call."

Fourth, participation in the call of God leads to what we will call "disciplined attachment." Purity of heart is to will one thing. Disciplined attachment aims at such a focus of one's freedom.

In the early stages of life we often find that doors open for us. Our elders and the society around us arrange possibilities for us. We are handed opportunities on a silver platter, as it were. As adults, however, we can no longer rely on doors opening for us. We must decide, most often with colleagues, what doors need to be opened. Then we plan, strategize, and act in concert to achieve the goals we aim at. In other words, instead of doors opening, one aims at opening doors.

In the course of such disciplined attachment one must be pragmatically flexible, willing to compromise and rethink strategy. Nevertheless, disciplined attachment means becoming concrete. It is relevant to family life as well as to work or political life. Being disciplined about religious education in the family is as much a virtue as being disciplined in political strategizing.

Furthermore, such attachment involves risk—one must commit oneself to a concrete course of action which will ruffle feathers. It involves ambiguity—one must say many noes for the sake of a few strong yeses. It involves using one's own critical intelligence as well as a willingness to live with the consequences of one's action. Perhaps Luther's advice to "sin boldly" sheds light on this aspect of the Christian's mission. One acts out one's intentional commitments boldly, with full knowledge that neither the internal motivation nor external effects of one's action will be pure or unambiguous. Nevertheless, one acts, and throws oneself on the mercy of God.

Finally, there is a companion to disciplined attachment in the faithful Christian's sense of call. That is "disciplined detachment." There often comes a time to release from attachments to particular jobs, institutions, causes, and even persons. (I am not counseling periodic divorce!) When "deep happiness" no longer meshes with the "deep hunger of the world," it may be time to move. There may be changes in the person that erode his or her "fit" with a particular role. The change may come in the institution or role. Or the needs of the world may change. What was once a dire need may have been addressed adequately while another dire need appears. Or, again, it may be that delicate whisper of the Spirit that calls a person to something new and different.

It is harmful to the Christian's mission to tarry too long. After all has been said and done, all poured out in "willing one thing," it may be time to move on both for the sake of the individual Christian and the institution. When "deep happiness" and "deep need" part company, effective mission is lost. Decisions of detachment should be disciplined, however. Mutual conversations with Christian brothers and sisters are most helpful and most necessary.

For example, after seventeen years of seminary teaching I felt my deep happiness and the school's deep need begin to part company. In many ways I thought I was not as effective in my call as I could be. My wife felt similarly. When an unexpected invitation was made by a church college to come there to teach, I discerned, with the counsel of several colleagues, the whisper of the Spirit to move. Even with all the trauma associated with such a decision, it was the right move. My call was renewed: the Spirit blew.

Summarizing, we can say that the appropriation of our justification by grace on account of Christ opens us to the Spirit's creative thrust. The righteousness of God in Christ, imparted by the Spirit, presses into our lives. It struggles with the Old Adam. It pushes for a new life in which we see the world differently. We see God at work in the places of responsibility that are ours. Those places take on a deeper meaning. But we also find our own call within that welter of worldly activity. Through a process of clarity about ourselves, expanded awareness of the world, focused intentionality, disciplined attachment and detachment, the Spirit begins to use us as a vehicle of God's purposes. Faith becomes active.

LOVE

Even though we have thus far pointed to a deeper dimension of worldly activities and have discussed our call within them, we have added no uniquely Christian *moral content* to those activities. An additional depth and seriousness are definitely there, but not any new moral direction. The homemaker, the elementary-school teacher, and the student can perform their roles with a heightened seriousness and joyfulness that attends faith, and yet express no transformative influence on those roles. If we go no further, the Christian faith could be accused of merely adding motivation to what the world holds as right and good. That is a formula for a very conservative social philosophy: Christians ought to do with joy what the worldly institutions tell them to do.

Without reneging from what we have already argued, it is necessary to complement the discussion of faith with that of love. Love is the transformative element, the leaven that leavens the lump.

Worldly existence certainly knows of many kinds of love. Libidinous love, erotic love, and filial love come to mind. All are characterized by a certain mutuality—one being has qualities that attract and complement another being. In the mutual exchange of these qualities, relationships of trust and loyalty are often built up. Persisting personal and communal relations emerge on the basis of mutuality. Higher forms of mutuality are the grounds of most expressions of covenantal existence. Rules are generally the formal means of identifying and shoring up these mutualities. Indeed, the places of responsibility we have previously examined are held together by the glue of mutuality, if not by mutual love then at least by mutual advantage or respect.

Christian love, however, is sharply different. It is not based on mutuality. It is based on the radical love that God showed in Jesus Christ. That love seeks us out, affirms us, and forgives us before any capacity or even inclination on our part to reciprocate that love. It upsets the nice calculus—the give and take—of mutual love. God's agape love in Christ is a kind of divine madness that breaks the sane confines of worldly love.

We can point to five characteristics of agape love that describe its quality. First, it is disinterested love. It loves without regard for the "value" of the other. The other may not be able or willing to contribute to the being of the lover by reciprocating. But the lover acts without guarantee of return, though she or he might wish for a return. The lover *initiates* care or concern for the other when the other cannot or will not respond mutually. The lover forgives the other without demanding repentance and mutual forgiveness.

Many teachings and actions of Jesus exhibit this disinterested quality. The Good Samaritan has mercy on the victim of robbery, continues to shower care upon him, and asks for no return. The father of the prodigal son spontaneously forgives. Ten lepers are healed although only one returns thanks. Agape love is expressed on the cross for all sinners, whether or not they respond in faith. Agape love is heedless; it does not calculate return.

A second quality of agape love is its universality. All beings are included within the orbit of divine love. Even the most despised are not excluded. Indeed, Jesus' ministry is a sustained attack on the barriers that limit God's love to a chosen few. His treatment of women, tax collectors, prostitutes, foreigners, and outcasts bears this out. The mission of the Christian movement is to bring the gospel of God's love to all people. The universal thrust of agape love is strikingly evident.

A third quality—agape's special concern for the vulnerable—may seem to be in some tension with its universality. It is again clear in Jesus' teaching and ministry that he gives special attention to the lost, last, and least. His mission is often to the poor. He shows mercy to the outcast. He forgives the grossest sinners. He heals lepers. This bias toward the vulnerable is so evident that theologies of liberation make it their center.

When one contemplates the love of God in Christ toward humanity, however, we *all* appear as outsiders and outcasts because of our willful disobedience. We have sentenced ourselves to the darkness and confusion of sinful existence. God's merciful love is especially concerned about all of us who are the lost, last, and least. So the vulnerable includes everyone even though they might not know how vulnerable they are.

This special concern for the vulnerable, the reality of which can be affirmed without denying the universality of agape, is like the love of parents for a sick child. The parents certainly love all their children, but yet will devote special effort and time to the sick one. That sick one will have the most obvious need and will know it. So it is with God's love; it aims especially at those oppressed with special needs.

Fourth, agape aims at the growth, healing, and inclusion into the bonds of mutuality for the other. Agape does not intend continuing dependency for the other. Rather, agape hopes, if at all possible, to bring the other to full human stature by contributing to its being. Peter is forgiven his cowardly betrayal not to make him a passive dependent on God's mercy but to free him for a vigorous mission on behalf of the church. Agape seeks the other's strong good, not fawning dependency on the lover's admirable generosity.

Finally, the expression of agape is often attended by suffering. Agape love is often sacrificial in character. This would not be the case were it not acting in a fallen world. The most dramatic demonstration that agape love becomes suffering love under the conditions of sin is the cross of Christ. A human life lived consistently out of agape love ended up on a cross. The qualities of love we have already discussed—its disinterestedness, universality, special concern for the vulnerable, and intentions for wholeness—were too threatening to too many people. Jesus' teaching and ministry affronted the nicely calculated give-and-take of spiritual and moral life. He simply represented too much radical generosity for people caught up in earning and flaunting their own esteem. In short, the embodiment of agape love entered into a context of alienated existence and became the target of the anger and wrath inevitably present in that alienation. The loving Christ places his life right in the midst of the angry gaps between humanity and God as well as among humans themselves. As Christ absorbs that anger in place of those who really deserve it, he suffers. At the same time, Christ as the representative of God takes into the divine life the wrath and judgment due us, the fallen creation.

But God's love in Christ, while sacrificial and suffering, is not defeated. The resurrection is the vindication of God's love as the most powerful and supreme reality. It is triumphant. Christ the king replaces the suffering Christ on the cross. While this victory will become complete only at the end of time, it was and is efficacious in human history. God's love in Christ heals, forgives, and renews those who receive it in faith. Likewise, human agape love heals, forgives, and renews human relationships that are constantly threatened by the destructive power of sin.

It is important to emphasize, however, that agape, expressed in Christ or in human actions, is never completely triumphant in history. The effects of sin are too stubbornly resistant for that. Sin has continuing power to frustrate and reject the aims of agape; therefore, agape love generally appears as suffering love, neither completely triumphant nor completely tragic.

If these five characteristics are at all descriptive of the kind of love taught and embodied by Jesus as God's Christ, it is clear that such love is in considerable tension with worldly loves, let alone the more self-interested actions that drive so many human activities. When Jesus' *religious* virtues, for example, "take no thought for the morrow," are combined with these moral virtues, one gets a very radical picture indeed. Its stark discontinuity with the world's ways becomes dramatically evident. Reinhold Niebuhr terms Jesus' religious and moral posture the "impossible possible." It was impossible because humans cannot live that way in the world without winding up on a cross. It was possible in that it was in fact done.

Such a life appears unworldly—indeed irresponsible—without an understanding of the unique vocation of Jesus. Jesus was not responsible to and for the partial interests and claims that give our lives their context and direction—family, work, citizenship, and the like. Jesus in fact stayed clear of such commitments. They would get him too deeply involved in the ambiguous claims and counterclaims of human interests. Thus, he joined no religious or political party. The Word and Deed of God in Christ had to come through clearly and purely, unencumbered by the distortions of human self-interest. Jesus as the Christ had to represent all persons before God, not just some. Conversely, he had to represent the purity of God's agape to all. God's love could not be refracted through other human agencies—religious or political. It had to be expressed by one man on a cross, deserted by all who would give that love their own distorted twist. The only passage from the All to all was through the solitary man on the cross.

We would be irresponsible, if not blasphemous, to imitate such a vocation. We are not called to represent all persons before God nor to redeem the whole creation through one decisive act of sacrificial love. We are to live as Christians in the limited and specific places of responsibility we have been given.

Yet, we are to reflect in some fashion the qualities of agape love in the limited conditions of our own lives. The love that saves and redeems us is the final truth about God and about life itself. We are called to live that truth, to shape our lives in consonance with the fundamental intentions of God.

But how? It should be clear by now that ordinary Christians find themselves in places of responsibility whose roles are shaped by decidedly worldly considerations. Responsible life in the family, at work, and in society entails excellences—skills and capabilities that are nonmoral in character. Furthermore, these institutions and their attendant roles are highly ambiguous. They are mixtures of creative and preservative impulses alongside destructive and idolatrous ones.

Even more significant is the fact that they are arranged so as to come to terms with our finitude and our sin. We are finite beings. We are first of all responsible to and for our own families; we cannot take direct responsibility for all the families in our neighborhood let alone in our country or the world. We are called to do our particular job, not someone or everyone else's. We are called, first of all, to be citizens of our own country, not another or all others. Our places of responsibility localize and particularize our efforts.

Moreover, these places of responsibility make us come to terms with our and the world's sin. We are pressured by various sanctions to fulfill our minimal responsibilities, even when our sinful selves pull in opposite directions. Also, institutions take into account the aggressiveness of the world's sin. A soldier or police officer must often use force or the threat of force to exercise their responsibilities. The business person must make hard-headed decisions in the face of stiff competition. Families protect themselves from intrusion or threat by adapting defensive measures.

Given our worldly existence, then, it is no simple thing to relate the radical love of God in Christ to our places of responsibility. The history of Christian churches is one long debate about whether and how that norm of radical love should relate to worldly existence. Truly, if we gaze honestly at the sublime radicality of God's love in Christ and the messiness and ambiguity of worldly responsibilities, we know it is no easy thing to proclaim ourselves followers of Christ. Anyone who claims too easily it is has either watered down the radicality of agape love or has viewed the world through rose-colored glasses. The cross is a dramatic reminder that Christ and the world—even at its best—do not fit smoothly together.

Some Christian traditions—which we earlier called "sectarian"—simply believe that one cannot be a follower of Christ and live in the world, particularly in those areas of worldly responsibility where power, coercion, and violence come into play. These Christians believe the world is so under the reign of evil and death that they must either withdraw from it or resist it. The older sectarian traditions, such as the Amish, construct their own Christian enclaves apart from the world while the new sectarians—evangelical groups like the Sojourners and individual writers like William Stringfellow, John Howard Yoder, and Stanley Hauerwas—are active in "exposing" the world's addiction to coercion and violence and demonstrating more "peaceable" ways. For these new sectarians, it is very difficult for Christians to be soldiers or to occupy positions of great economic or political power.

A much more common, but less admirable, response to the terrific tension between the radical norm of agape and the ambiguities of worldly responsibility is to deny the relevance of Christian agape love to worldly existence, particularly in its public and social dimensions. Mistaken interpretations of the Lutheran "two-kingdoms" doctrine periodically make this denial. That classical Lutheran teaching argues that God reigns in the world in two distinct ways—by the law, which involves the use of power, and by the gospel, which promises the grace of God to sinners who then, insofar as they live out of that grace, freely and spontaneously do God's will in the world. This Lutheran perspective in fact provides the framework for the entire argument of this book.

But this "two-kingdoms" approach can and has been distorted. When Christians argue, as some of them have in Germany, Chile, and South Africa, that the love of God in Christ has no connection with the political struggle for a more just society, they exemplify this kind of distortion. Thereby they deny that God makes demands for justice on our worldly institutions that Christians, responding to God's agape, must take seriously. They leave the world to its own guidance system, which is disastrous.

This particular Lutheran distortion is manifested much more massively in those many Christians who practically divorce their daily lives from the impingement of agape love. For too many "business is business," and they do not allow Christian love any role in worldly affairs, except perhaps in their more intimate relations. They separate Sunday from Monday.

An opposite way of breaking the tension between agape and our worldly patterns pretends that agape can offer *direct* guidance for our life in society, economics, and politics. Rather than keeping Sunday separate from Monday, it tries to make Monday into Sunday. That is, this approach sentimentally believes that the radical qualities of agape love can govern social, economic, and political life. The banker, for example, can deny the stringent criteria of credit-worthiness in approving loans and simply give money to the most vulnerable. Or, the statesperson can give up worrying about balances of power among nations and pursue policies of unilateral disarmament.

Such approaches break the tension by commending an irresponsible openness. Requirements built into one's place of responsibility are simply neglected. The results of such an approach would be grim. The banker would either lose her or his job or the bank would fall into bankruptcy. The statesperson would allow international life to be determined by the strongest and most aggressive nations. In either case, the world in all its ambiguous toughness is not taken seriously.

A fourth way of escaping the tension between agape and worldly life is to separate Christians into two basic classes. This was the approach of Catholicism for many centuries. The clergy—particularly the monastics—were expected to live up to the radical qualities of agape. The laity in the world were expected to live up to a less heroic standard—natural law. It should be emphasized, though, that the requirements of natural law prevented daily life from being simply given over to the world's devices. In recent years, however, Catholics have distanced themselves from the old model by challenging the laity with a higher vision.

The Lutheran and Calvinist reformers, at their best, did not break the tension in the relations of agape and worldly existence. Luther, for example, placed that tension right in the heart of the Christian layperson. Each Christian at one and the same time is to be responsible to the claims of his or her own worldly role *and* to the lure of agape love. Reinhold Niebuhr, many centuries later, proposed a similar approach. He argued that the radical ethical norm of agape interacts dialectically with the norms and demands associated with our worldly places of responsibility. There is a lively no and yes in relation to them. Agape love—characterized by the qualities we discussed earlier—serves as:

1. indeterminate judgment of all our worldly patterns;
2. indeterminate possibility, that is, it challenges every pattern to higher moral attainment;

3. discriminate judgment—it helps us make selective assessments of given worldly patterns; and

4. a transcendent standard that persuades us of our shortcomings and faults.

What does all this mean practically? It means that each Christian, precisely within the places of responsibility, responds to a *special moral summons.* Nurtured in the Christian story, the Christian is motivated toward the quality of God's love in Christ—agape love. Besides this dispositional orientation, the Christian may also hold before her or him the qualities of agape as standards or norms. Those qualities may be looked upon as ideals toward which to aim.

Then the struggle begins. Our places of responsibility, with their sanctions and ambiguities, hold us to particular roles that move toward closure, toward the "ethics of defense." We cannot escape these particularized and defensive elements in our role. But yet agape draws us out of closure. Agape's disinterestedness, universality, and bias toward the vulnerable stretches us toward openness. Agape lures us out of our ethics of defense. Christian vocation maintains the creative tension between the concrete demands of one's place of responsibility and the lure of agape. The Christian is called to a continuous renegotiation of the balance between taking the world as it is and moving it toward a more compassionate and more inclusive community of being.

This calls for aiming at the *fitting action*—that which takes seriously what the world requires *and* yet stretches toward what agape requires. The deed emerges somewhere on a continuum between complete closure and complete openness. It is the creative work of the Christian person in the midst of the ambiguities of the world. It qualifies and enriches worldly morality.

The motivation and/or ideal of agape is therefore a constant qualification of our worldly morality. Agape does not allow us to become complacent—it ferrets out the taint and distortion in our every motive and deed. It calls us to richer and broader moral possibilities. It helps us decide between specific courses of action, and it encourages a spirit of contrite humility. It is the salt that provides the savor.

Let us look at a concrete example. This is the story of an art teacher confronted with a problem student "dumped" into her class for want of anything else to do with him. Jimmy flunked the art class without handing in any work at all during the term. In the process he created havoc in the class. The next year Jimmy approached the teacher about taking art again.

The teacher continues her story:

I said no way. He had caused me enough grief the previous year and I certainly didn't need another year of him disrupting class. I was teaching in the main building and my planning period coincided with Jimmy's study hall. The study halls were large and noisy. Jimmy came by the room one day and asked could he come in there to study rather than go to his normal study hall class. I told him as long as he planned to study and got permission from his teacher, it was okay with me. Before long a few more students had joined Jimmy and we had our own smaller study hall in my room.

As time passed, Jimmy began to talk to me and to ask if there was anything he could do to help me. I knew enough about him to be hesitant to say yes, but then decided maybe he needed someone to trust him and to give him some responsibilities. I began by giving him small things to do and as the year progressed gave him more and more. Not once did he ever make a mistake or refuse to do what I asked him. He did his work and was a tremendous help to me.

The last week of school we always had an assembly program at which the seniors read their last will and testament. When Jimmy got up to read his, he looked straight at me and left me his undying friendship. Needless to say, I was shocked and know there must have been tears in my eyes. Here was a student I had refused to let take art but who in the past year had come to consider me his friend. That made all the heartache worthwhile and I've often wondered what happened to Jimmy and what he is doing now.

True to life, the story has no triumphant end with Jimmy going on to be president of IBM. But his chances of making a decent way in the world were enhanced by that ordinary saint. It seems that all the qualities of agape love are present in that Christian teacher's action toward Jimmy. At the same time she took the requirements and standards of her job seriously. She was not sentimental or permissive. She stuck to her guns.

If she did only what her job required, however, Jimmy's life would have been distinctly impoverished. Instead she "stretched" her role. Her action was the leaven that leavened the lump of Jimmy's life. It helped to heal a wounded part of God's creation. Christian love is like a silken, scarlet thread that binds together the fabric of God's tapestry which is constantly under threat of tearing apart because of sin and evil.

In such an example, which can be duplicated by the thousands among the ordinary saints of God, the Spirit works through Christians to heal and restore the world. Through this "service to all" the world is moved a bit closer toward the intentions of God. As Christians participate in this work of the Spirit, they often experience suffering. As Luther noted, Christians need not seek the cross in their calling; the cross will find them if the special lure of agape is taken seriously. The "stretching" will be painful. But it will be a theonomous echo of that embodied love that was stretched on a cross twenty centuries ago.

Every calling in every place of responsibility provides occasions for responding to the lure of agape. No one can plead the lack of opportunity. Moreover, those occasions are not simply the prerogatives of Lone-Ranger Christians. They are part of the life of Christian communities and churches. Likewise, those communities support and guide individuals as they live in that creative tension between closure and openness. Those on the firing line are driven back to the nurture of the community and its faith as they work out their callings.

HOPE

We have argued that the work of the Spirit through us in our callings opens the eyes of faith to deeper levels of meaning in our ordinary responsibilities as well as to our own particular mission within those responsibilities. The Spirit working through us also involves a special moral summons—that of agape love. Insofar as we are enabled to grow in faith and love we move toward theonomy. We become transparent to God's purposes in the world. We participate in the creative, governing, and healing activity of God. Our bodies become a "living sacrifice, holy and acceptable to God."

Transparency is a double-edged sword, however. Besides revealing the divine activity, it also reveals the persisting flaws of self and world. The light that is strong enough to shine through our resistant being highlights the pattern of our resistance as well. Hope, if it is to be solid, must take into account the persisting sin in self and world. And since our sin is at root a willful separation from God, we must begin our discussion of hope with a consideration of our personal relation to God. Without continuing trust and confidence in God, there is little for us to hope for.

OUR BEING IN RELATION TO GOD

Authentic hope is able to be sustained in the face of those stark realities that tend to dash it. If it cannot be sustained in those conditions, it is little more than shallow optimism. Christians are up against those stark realities just like others. In fact, they may bear greater burdens because their conception of their responsibility may be broader and deeper.

Like others, Christians are pressed by the force of external demands. The claims of the family and/or work are often strong enough to destroy our capacity for adequate response. It is not unusual for businesses to demand too much of their employees. Any parent can recount the perplexity of how to respond to rebellious children. Taken together, this whole system of callings can exert so much pressure that persons are driven to distraction.

Each stage of moral development carries with it an implicit crisis. The egoist is finally pushed up against her or his own impotence and guilt, the heteronomist sooner or later recognizes that the group has feet of clay up to its neck, and the autonomist will come to see that even the most creative practical intelligence cannot measure up to the challenges of the whole picture.

Further, those with a specific sense of Christian calling will be aware of how they fall short of both the mission they have been called to and the special moral summons they have been given. All Christians are driven by their involvement in finite and sinful existence into a sense of helplessness and worthlessness before the transcending task that is theirs. They are aware of the inadequacy of both the motives and effects of their action.

With such a sense of the stark realities of responsible life in the world, it is quite possible to despair rather than hope. Often I have left a classroom wondering if anything I said was of value to the students. In my darker moments I wonder what, if anything, my calling as a teacher has wrought. It seems so meager considering the opportunities I have been given. At moments like that we are all tempted to become paralyzed by our sense of guilt for our failures.

We can become obsessed with our struggling selves. We wonder whether we can muster enough confidence to go on.

Here it is that the promise of God's justifying grace in Christ gives precisely that hope that fires our motivation to go on. The Christian life begins and ends in the grace of God. That is, we are not finally justified before God by how well we in fact perform our callings. We are affirmed, accepted, and forgiven by God's graceful judgment, not by our own weak responses.

What a comfort that is! What grounds for hope! If our ultimate worth, our personal relation to God, is not dependent on our efforts but on God's faithfulness, then we can pick up our lives and live them anew every morning. We need not fear failure even as we try to succeed. The most important thing—our acceptance by God—does not hang on our success. With that assurance, we can go on our way, full of hope and grief.

Now that is good news. It is not the kind of news the world gives. And the hope ignited by the gospel is not a hope that the world can give either. It is not built on the unsure affirmations of others. Nor is it a cheap hope. It only comes to us when we have struggled with the intractabilities of our and the world's sins. "Our hope is built on nothing less than Jesus' blood and righteousness." God's grace makes us free and hopeful lords of all even as we are faltering servants of all.

OUR ACTIONS IN RELATION TO HISTORY

A second set of realities tends to dash our hope and debilitate our moral resolve. We know that both the motive and the effects of our action are mixed. If we are honest with ourselves we must admit that we are never certain about why we do things. Part of our motive may be altruistic but upon closer scrutiny we find we often act because we will look good to the significant others around us. We often get ego strokes for our good deeds and find ourselves wondering whether we would act thusly without those strokes. A good deal of the time we must struggle with ourselves in order to do the minimally good or right, let alone what agape would summon. It seems that every act is damaged by the mixed motives that lie behind it. A pure will is indeed an elusive thing.

On the other side of the action equation, we are aware of the ambiguity of effects. The more we take on responsible roles, the more our every major deed carries negative as well as positive effects. When we discipline our children we know that some psychic damage is done along with the necessary civilizing function. When someone is hired, the joyful occasion is marred by the awareness that other candidates have been turned down. When persons achieve roles that involve great power, the ambiguity quotient goes up along with the power. With full knowledge of the horrendous effects of the atomic bombs, Harry Truman decided to drop them on Hiroshima and Nagasaki because he was convinced that in the long run such action would save lives. Talk about ambiguity!

At this point we must again emphasize the importance of justification by grace, not works. We have already affirmed that in the preceding section. But we are not only concerned about ourselves before God, we are also concerned about the effects of our actions in history. What can redeem them from their ambiguity?

With regard to this challenge we can only hope in the sovereignty of God. No one can gauge the motives or effects of human action, neither those of the self nor of others. Actions emerge from mysterious springs and have unforeseen and long-persisting effects. If we think we can control either we err. Such a claim leads to arrogance and then soon to despair. Rather, we act with the best motives we can summon and toward the best ends we can perceive, but leave the final results up to the Lord of history. It is simply not all up to us. Our actions can and will be used as the Lord sees fit. God will receive them and place them into the complex economy of his history. In the end we will see how God used them, but for now we see only through a very dark glass. Our hope is in the sovereignty of God, not in our own actions.

Besides the ambiguity of motive and effect, another threatening reality can be met only by Christian hope. That is the reality of our obscurity in history. In moments of clarity we become aware of our obscurity. A few minutes in a country churchyard brings such clarity. There, and in hundreds of thousands of cemeteries around the world, the ordinary saints of God gradually disappear from human memory. Not only do they disappear, but their deeds of love are also forgotten.

Though the parental love of my great-grandparents no doubt has an indirect effect on me through my grandparents (whom I remember) and my parents, they and their loving deeds are certainly obscure.

A few of the heroes of the faith are etched fairly permanently in the churches' memory. That is good and important—we need exemplars to serve as beacons for our moral and spiritual lives. But for every one of those there are a million who were exemplars in a much more limited way and who are now forgotten. For each of those there are millions more whose loving actions were only fleetingly remembered, if at all. Many lived out their Christian lives, however imperfectly, in pervasive obscurity.

It is a chilling prospect to think that their lives and deeds have disappeared without a trace, except for those isolated wisps of life long past that are detected by social historians. Such is the prospect for us in most of our secular philosophies of history. But Christians have a different view.

One of the most important days of the church year is All Saints' Sunday, when heroes *and* ordinary saints are celebrated. There we affirm that all the saints, the obscure among them, are "hid with God." They make up the invisible cloud of witnesses present at the Eucharist. Their loving actions are not lost in the empty halls of history, nor are they dependent on our memories. Their deeds mean something to God and his purposes, regardless of their reception or retention here on earth. The transcendent ground from which their loving deeds proceeded also envelops them forever.

Thus, the steadfast sovereignty of God is the ground of Christian hope with regard to the ambiguity and obscurity of our actions in the world. We can act with confident hope that our actions, though ambiguous and obscure, mean something at a level beyond history. They are gathered into God's story, which, though not evident to us or to the world, is one finally of grace, not judgment. Ordinary saints can live and love with confidence that their lives and deeds are not brief flickers in a vast, dark universe, but are living reflections of the perpetual light of God which will never be lost.

THE FUTURE

The moral relevance of hope cannot be confined to the personal dimension that we have explored. Concern for the future not only includes attention to the motives and effects of our action, as well as its obscurity, but also to the whole of humankind and the whole of history. Without that universal thrust, Christian hope becomes anemic indeed, if not downright selfish. Authentic hope includes hope for the fulfillment of all things.

Our twentieth-century experience has dashed the brief flurry of optimism that flourished in the eighteenth and nineteenth centuries. We no longer believe in automatic progress fueled by scientific and technological advance and guided by reason. All those agencies can be used for death-dealing as well as life-giving purposes. In fact, the most compelling view of the future for those concerned about it is a kind of secular apocalypticism. Book after book, movie after movie detail the horrors of nuclear holocaust. For them universal death is right around the corner. If that happens, all is lost.

Christians do not see it that way. Nor do they believe in utopian hopes in their progressive guises. We are sure about two things. First, we know that the temporal end to our personal life and to our world will come before their fulfillment is reached. The eschatological and apocalyptic teachings of the Bible, as well as our own historical background, bear that out. The forces of sin and evil are persistent and real enough to blunt any notion of fulfillment through human efforts in this world. Those forces must be overcome by some power beyond the human project itself.

The second certainty is that God *will* bring about the fulfillment of his kingdom. We know not when or how, nor do we know exactly what that kingdom will be like, except that its content will be consistent with the love of God revealed in Jesus. The power that resurrected Jesus is working in us and in the world. God is drawing all of being to himself. The future is God's.

The point of transition between these two certainties—that the world cannot and will not complete itself and that God will bring it about—entails death and judgment. We face those before the kingdom comes. And they make us shudder.

But we can hope. Christians believe that Jesus will be their representative before the judgment seat of God. And they will be pronounced righteous on account of Christ. But Christian hope is more expansive than that. The love that is revealed in Christ is the final word about God's character and intentions. No one and nothing will be finally lost. All will be judged in a fitting way, but God's love will finally triumph.

There is a marvelous scene in Flannery O'Connor's short story "Revelation" where the terror and hope of the final day are portrayed. The lame and halt, the freaks and misfits, the respectable and the elite, the old and young, all process grandly upward on a great bridge of light to heaven. Some stride with dignity. Some hop like frogs. But all bear a fiery trail behind them in which the dross of their sin and corruption is burned away. It must be painful indeed. But the eyes of all the faithful are shining with hope as God draws them upward.

The future is in God's good hands. Christians need not fear. We can plant trees in our gardens even while the world is paralyzed with apocalyptic fear. We can work for the relative improvements in historical life that are so important, without being addicted to promises of human utopias. We can face our own ends, as well as the world's, with a serenity borne of hope. We do not have the final word nor does the world. God does.

In summary, then, places of responsibility become Christian callings when Christians in them express the Spirit working through them in faith, love, and hope. Then, responsible life manifests a holy secularity. Faith brings a deeper meaning to worldly responsibilities as well as an individual sense of mission or vocation within them. Love brings a special moral summons that stretches those responsibilities outward to and for a universe of being and inward to and for the most vulnerable among us. Hope enables us to continue to act with vigor in spite of continued sin, ambiguity of motive and effect, obscurity and uncertainty about the movement of history.

Faith, love, and hope are consequences of the grace of God in Jesus Christ. They follow God's initiative in Christ; they do not elicit it, for it is there all the time. The Spirit working in us opens us to faith in that grace and the Spirit working through us brings forth the fruit of that faith.

The subtitle of this chapter—*'toward* theonomy"—is meant to emphasize that theonomy is not ours to possess. When it appears in our life it is the gift of the Spirit. The righteousness of Christ that is given for our justification becomes active in our moral lives. There is no guarantee, however, that the Old Adam in us will simply step aside to let that righteousness flow. In fact, we can be sure of the opposite. The struggle between old and new will continue until the end. We will always be justified and sinner at the same time. Honest Christians will know that every day they will oscillate between the old and new; they will find themselves each day at several points on the continuum of moral development. Egoism and heteronomy will not disappear. Indeed, Christians are aware that the righteous know they are not righteous.

Nevertheless, we aim for growth. But we can aim for growth in faith, love, and hope only by attending to the nurture of our Christian being, both individually and in the company of other Christians. If we are to "die and rise daily with Christ," we need the sustenance of Christian devotion, prayer, fellowship, and worship. Above all we need to hear the Word of God and receive the sacraments. Christian calling leads inevitably to Christian nurture.

BIBLIOGRAPHY

On the Lutheran doctrine of vocation:

Billing, Einar. *Our Calling.* Rock Island, Ill.: Augustana, 1951.

Bonhoeffer, Dietrich. *Ethics.* New York: Macmillan Co.; London: SCM Press, 1955.

Buechner, Frederick. *Wishful Thinking: A Theological ABC.* New York: Harper & Row, 1973.

Forde, Gerhard. "Christian Life." In *Christian Dogmatics,* edited by Carl E. Braaten and Robert W. Jenson, 2:391–469. Philadelphia: Fortress Press, 1984.

Forell, George. *Faith Active in Love.* Minneapolis: Augsburg, 1954.

Heiges, Donald. *The Christian's Calling.* Rev. ed. Philadelphia: Fortress Press, 1984.

Lazareth, William. *Luther on the Christian Home: An Application of the Social Ethics of the Reformation.* Philadelphia: Muhlenberg Press, 1960.

Luther, Martin. "The Freedom of the Christian." In *Martin Luther: Selections from His Writings,* edited by John Dillenberger. Garden City, N.Y.: Doubleday Anchor Books, 1961.

Wingren, Gustaf. *Luther on Vocation.* Philadelphia: Muhlenberg Press, 1957.

On the relation of agape love to worldly activity:

Niebuhr, H. Richard. *Christ and Culture.* New York: Harper & Brothers, 1951.

Niebuhr, Reinhold. *An Interpretation of Christian Ethics.* New York: Harper & Row, 1979.

————. *The Nature and Destiny of Man: A Christian Interpretation.* New York: Charles Scribner's Sons, 1941.

On hope:

Braaten, Carl. *The Future of God: The Revolutionary Dynamics of Hope.* New York: Harper & Row, 1969.

Pannenberg, Wolfhart. *Theology and the Kingdom of God.* Philadelphia: Westminster Press, 1969.

Schwarz, Hans. "Eschatology." In *Christian Dogmatics,* ed. Braaten and Jenson, 2:471–587.

PART
III

THE CALLINGS OF
THE CHRISTIAN

I therefore, a prisoner for the Lord, beg you to lead a life worthy of the
calling to which you have been called.

(Ephesians 4:1)

The general, overarching calling of each Christian is made concrete
in specific callings. God the Spirit works through us to serve others
in particular places of responsibility. Part 3 will deal with those
particular places—marriage and family life (chap. 7), work (chap. 8),
public life (chap. 9), and religious life (chap. 10).

Each chapter will examine how the Christian life is expressed in
these particular places. In each instance there will be an effort to
delineate the particular set of principles or ends that ought to guide
each sphere of responsible life. Such efforts are gropings after the
Creator's intentionality that governs and orders particular spheres of
responsibility. In view of the encrustation of social sanctions, the
dynamism and ambiguity of each place of responsibility, there is
indeed room for humility about our capacity to know God's will. In
addition to those characteristics the transcendent mystery of the
divine intentionality itself prohibits easy identification. Premature
claims to discern God's will should be discouraged.

Nevertheless, the Christian community is not without guidance in
these matters. The accumulation of human historical experience
sheds some light on how human life is best ordered. We also have
our own Christian communal and individual experience of and re-

flection on God's intentions for human life. Above all, we have the
Scriptures as a guide to God's basic intentions. While it is certainly
true that God brings forth new things in history so that "time makes
ancient good uncouth," we trust that those new things are consonant
with the basic thrust of God's will as it is revealed in Scripture.

After attending to the guiding principles and ends for each place
of responsibility, which reflect the moral governance of God the
Creator, we shall examine the particular contributions of Christian
faith, love, and hope to responsible life in each place. In this way we
shall see how common human responsibility becomes a Christian
calling. Or, putting it another way, we shall see how the special grace
of God in Christ elicits Christian responses of faith, love, and hope
that enrich, restore, and heal a world that has fallen away from the
Creator's governance.

7

Marriage and Family Life

And the two shall become one flesh.
(Mark 10:8)

Rich and stable marriage and family life are two of the greatest blessings we human creatures can receive. Among all else they indeed make life a joy and delight. Yet those gifts, if torn apart by sin or misfortune, can turn to occasions of bitter regret. As the *Lutheran Book of Worship* has it, "the gladness of marriage can be overcast and the gift of the family can become a burden." Sadly enough, all too many marriages are ending in that bitter regret and far too many families are being shattered by marital breakup.

The present situation regarding marriage and family life exemplifies the ambiguities of the modern world which we analyzed in chapter 1. The benefits and threats of modernity, as well as its pervasive confusion, are easily discernible in the plight of contemporary marriage and family life.

As technical reason has been applied productively to the material conditions of life, living standards have risen dramatically. Married couples and their children are not harnessed to permanent patterns of drudgery that snuff out the creative and expansive possibilities of life. They now have the resources to pursue goals far beyond mere survival. Moreover, couples can now plan and limit their families by using contraceptive technology. Medical advance fosters greater longevity, health, and vitality. And not least, technical progress at least partly liberates men and women from roles defined by physical capacities and thereby encourages more equality.

The application of historical reason has also brought benefits to marriage and family life. We no longer need to mistake nineteenth-century patterns of patriarchal and authoritarian marriage and family arrangements as God's eternal will. Our awareness of human relativity has introduced some refreshing openness and flexibility into marital and familial life.

The liberal spirit has bestowed much autonomy to married couples and families. They have become increasingly free from social pressures and traditions that formerly dictated how they should live their lives. The freedom my married daughter has in comparison to what my parents had is immense. She and her husband can adopt just about any life style they choose—something out of the question in my parents' day. Indeed, the liberal elaboration of rights within marriage and family life has bestowed both protection and autonomy on individuals, couples, and families.

Even the ethic of self-enhancement has contributed something. Partners in a marriage and members of a family are more willing to assert their own interests than in an earlier day. This has probably brought about more equality in marriage and family life and it has certainly enabled people to break out of destructive relationships that would simply have had to have been endured a generation ago. The concern for "personal happiness" is not always negative. Secularization has diminished the heavy taboos surrounding the breaking of marriage vows, controlling conception, the practice of abortion, homosexual activity, and sexual conduct in general. This has widened the space for human choice and expressiveness.

The negative effects of modernity, however, complicated by the perennial pressures of human sin, are as dramatic as the benefits. The pace and pervasiveness of social change fueled by technological change have exerted tremendous pressures on marriage and family. Constant movement, the disruption of conventional patterns, and the unrelenting hecticness of life in modern Western society buffet even the most solid marriages and families. The rising living standards made possible by technical advance lure people toward an undue regard for comfort, pleasure, and entertainment, and from attention to values of sacrifice and discipline which hold these fundamental units together.

Historical reason, while paving the way for more openness, flexibility, and equality, also fosters a kind of normlessness that is as confusing as it is liberating. Marriage is whatever two persons say it is. Family is any kind of social arrangement in which people gather under the same roof. Indeed, when President Carter called his conference on family life, it almost broke up in bickering about the definition of the family. "Alternative" marriage and family arrangements are not only defended as morally tolerable, they are often celebrated as improvements on the repressions of "bourgeois" conventionality. The fringes of women's and sexual liberation groups glory in the demolition of the old ways but have little to supply as a concrete vision for the future. Even the church subverts its own norms by its well-intentioned efforts to affirm persons in whatever fractured circumstances they find themselves.

The liberal spirit, combined with the acids of historical reason, has helped to undercut the social structures of marriage and family life by elevating a highly individualistic, rational calculation into them. Marriages become agreed-upon contracts—either formal or informal—which purport to stipulate the intricate mutualities of marital life. Family life is subjected to cost-benefit analysis. In both cases a strict and rational reciprocity is aimed at. When that reciprocity breaks down, the agreement goes with it. Further, the social cohesion and accountability associated with the traditional structures are often ignored by the private autonomy of couples and the families they produce. Why not live together if we like each other and it provides mutual benefits? Why marry and get involved in possible legal entanglements? Why have children legitimately if there are no social repercussions for not doing so?

Under these conditions the easy private decision by which persons involve themselves in life together is matched by the easy private decision to disband it. It is as though highly variegated individual parts of an intricate machine are restlessly but unsuccessfully in search of a perfect fit with other equally variegated parts. Add to this the uncompromising thrust of the self-enhancement ethic, which asserts its own claim for sexual, professional, and personal fulfillment, and one has the formula for highly unstable bonding. Further, when fulfillment is defined in materialistic or at least hedonistic terms, the restless search for new pleasures discourages the daunting task of coming to terms with a spouse or with family members over the long run.

The secularization that attends the dominance of technical and historical reason, the liberal spirit, and the self-enhancement ethic contributes to the general instability and confusion surrounding marriage and family life. Marriage vows are seen less and less as sacred vows before God. Rather, they are conditional agreements between consenting adults. Rites of marriage become attractive social ornaments to satisfy the need for some public and communal dimension to the liaison that has already been going on. Sexual intercourse becomes the occasion for pleasurable and mutual self-fulfillment bereft of sacramental significance, be it interpersonal or progenerational. Thus, the constraints of sacred meaning systems are loosened and human will flows according to its desire.

Of course, the negative portrait just sketched is a caricature of reality. It would apply only to the worst cases. Most of the searching unmarrieds, the struggling marrieds, and the already divorced are caught between the positive and negative polarities of modernity, between the older order and the newer disorder. They grope with anguish and joy toward some resolution that is personally satisfying and responsible. But, unfortunately, the number of failures in reaching such a resolution seems to be growing.

Thus, it is important that guidance and nurture be offered in a time of great confusion and struggle. The following represents a Christian effort to do just that. In it we will move from a discussion of marriage and family life as a place of responsibility to an illumination of them as Christian callings in which responsibilities are transformed by faith, love, and hope.

MARRIAGE AND FAMILY LIFE AS
A PLACE OF RESPONSIBILITY

As we have argued earlier, the major places of responsibility in which we live our lives are guided ultimately by the divine intention that is always in tension with the human propensity for sin. That divine intention is reflected imperfectly by social sanctions which are efforts to come to terms with both the underlying divine intention and human disorder. All of this is worked out in the ever-increasing dynamic of the modern world.

The underlying intention of marriage and family life is partially grasped in the long story of human experience as it has worked toward more fulfilling human relationships. It is more definitively reflected in the history of Jewish and Christian communities as they have developed their visions of marriage and family life, and as those visions have shaped the broader social life of the West. The core of those visions has been located in the sacred scriptures of those communities.

Consonant with historical experience, Jewish and Christian history and scripture, marriage is governed toward three ends: a lifelong covenant of fidelity between two persons; the bearing and nurture of children; and partnership in a broader mission in the world.

LIFELONG COVENANT OF FIDELITY

It is natural for persons to be mutually attracted to one another. It is particularly natural for young men and women to be attracted to each other. Often such attractions are initially based on romantic considerations—each "only has eyes" for the other. Mutualities are wider and firmer than the romantic, though. Young persons become friends—they mutually complement each other by the excellences of their character. They delight in and are nurtured by each other's presence. This is a much firmer mutuality. Other mutualities also apply. The couple may be interested in the same values and causes. They may find it pragmatically useful to be together; it is often economically advantageous to marry. They may simply have a lot of fun together. And of course there is sexual attraction, which runs all through the mutualities already mentioned but also transcends them all. Sexual attraction is a powerful motor of mutuality.

These mutualities, while necessary as the foundation of a lifelong covenant of fidelity, are only partially and fragilely formed. They need the shelter of promise in order to grow and flourish. The more permanent and unconditional the promise, the more likely it is that two persons can grow together. They can count on one another and therefore be vulnerable to each other. Further, the more that promise is shored up by public, communal support, the more likely it is that the promise will be kept. Therefore, weddings in all societies are the occasion of public ceremony and celebration.

As the promise is made, loyalties shift from friends and family to spouse. Responsibilities to and for the partner are worked out. In this time of fluidity of sexual roles, such responsibilities take more negotiation and compromise than before. But they certainly include economic, householding, and child-raising dimensions. Fidelity includes commitment to the spouse as the first human loyalty of life, sexual exclusiveness, and a willingness to be with and for the other in all the ups and downs of life.

Such a lifelong covenant of fidelity provides not only the optimal context for the most fulfilling interpersonal mutualities, it has the important byproduct of being a school for personal development. Within that sustained unity in duality, each person has the opportunity, indeed, the necessity, to practice patience, consideration, compromise, sacrifice, sensitivity, and kindness. In short, persons learn to love in a mature way. As persons learn mature love for one another their promises are strengthened and deepened. They practice the most serious kind of promise-making and -keeping.

CHILDREN

A second end of marriage is the bearing and nurturing of children. A stable and happy marriage is obviously the best place for the birth and care of new human creatures. The travails of one-parent families—particularly those of the very young and poor—are bringing that truism home to us powerfully.

The raising of children is a huge challenge. It promises heavy responsibility as well as plenteous delight. Those partners in a solid marriage are best prepared for the task. Therefore, while it may be a general obligation to have and raise children, there are circumstances that justify exceptions to the rule. Instability in marriage is one. A couples' heavy concentration on worthy callings or causes outside the home may be another. Obvious shortcomings in personal character yet another.

But, barring those exceptions, marriage certainly should aim at the bearing and nurture of children. Bearing them, with all its attendant hazards and joys, is fairly obvious. Nurturing them is not. In fact, the topsy-turvy logic of our contemporary world seems to have lost sight of the paramount importance of nurture. In the rush of each partner to have a career, children get lost in the shuffle. They are brought up with too much reliance on day care, baby sitters, and relatives. Later on they are left to fend for themselves, with typically unfortunate results. The young are simply not the object of enough nurture, generally speaking.

If nurturing is taken seriously, time and effort must be devoted in a disciplined fashion to providing children with a sustained, orderly, and secure environment of love. Within that environment they are taught the practices of civilized life, of virtues like honesty, compassion, and responsibility, and of worthy purposes toward which life should be lived. Above all they must be affirmed as significant participants in the family.

BROADER MISSION

As families form children of excellent character, a highly important task is performed for the broader society. Not only is a stable and happy marriage in itself a boon to society since it produces stable and happy persons, the children that issue from such a context are even more of a benefit. They will be the ones that replenish and guide the society of the future. Instead of being a problem for the society, they will enrich it. The energy of those children will be freed for service to others rather than to obsession with their damaged selves. Properly functioning families are primal models of self-government that make it possible for the larger society to engage in self-government.

Mission to the broader world takes on other dimensions also. Increasingly in our day it includes care for aging parents who earlier on had invested themselves in the nurture of their children. It also includes providing a support base for other callings of family members—work, public, and church life. All serious forays into the outer world are made easier by solid, orderly, and supportive family life.

Finally, the family's broader mission frequently aims at fostering values and causes in the outer world that are shared by the family. It is a rare family indeed that cannot find commonly held values that they can support in a coordinated way. For example, some families might take a special interest in supporting scouting or youth activities in the church or a particular political cause like conservation. As directors of voluntary organizations know, such families are crucial to their viability. They provide money, time, and leadership for the organization.

MARRIAGE AS A
CHRISTIAN CALLING

Thus far we have outlined purposes for marriage and family life that would receive wide affirmation from Western persons, whether Christian or not. The Jewish and Christian visions of marriage and family life have had a powerful impact on broader societal ideals. It is true that those ideals are under fire from a minority of critics who consider those notions too restrictive. It is even more true that our Western practice has departed severely from those ideals. Our marriage failure rate is pushing toward the 50-percent mark, and the incidence of marital breakup among Christian people, even the clergy, does not vary all that much from the general rate. Extramarital and premarital sex have increased. More children are being brought up in one-parent families. All families are finding it harder to maintain their cohesiveness.

Confusion and disorder are painfully evident. All the more important, then, that a clear, specific notion of Christian marriage be affirmed, for the good of both church and society. All the more important, too, that a common place of responsibility—marriage and family life—be illuminated by Christian faith, love, and hope, and thereby be transformed into a Christian calling.

FAITH

It is important to reaffirm that the central focus of Christian faith is the grace of God in Christ, which justifies and frees. It is through that gracious gift that we glimpse the heart of God and are able to view all of life as gift. The special grace of God in Christ awakens us through the Spirit to appropriate God's common grace in all of life.

One of the effects of God's liberating grace, we earlier argued, is the capacity to see a deeper dimension to life in our places of responsibility. The goodness of that life is received as gift, and the Source of the gift is known, thanked, and joyfully obeyed.

Such is certainly true of marriage and family life. The three purposes we elaborated above are not viewed simply as results of the evolutionary process, as purely human constructions, or as products of necessary repression for the sake of an orderly civilization. While those purposes can to some extent be attributed to the causes just mentioned, Christian eyes see something deeper. Those three purposes are grounded in the intentions of God. Indeed the institution of marriage is a "holy estate." The lifelong covenant of fidelity is established by God as a way of founding human community. When we live in accordance with that establishment, we move with God's will; when we ignore or violate it, we rebel against something more than human convention.

It is a great blessing in our marriages and in our families to know that we are "walking in the way of the Lord" when we keep the covenant of fidelity with spouse and family. The sacred canopy hallows our life together, shielding us from the confusion and disorder of the world.

The holy estate of marriage and its attendant family life, however, are not viewed only as locations of God's sacred presence in general, they are locations where *I,* with all my particularity, may find a calling, a summons from God. In order to discern and decide about such a calling, the four steps that were suggested earlier will be helpful.

First, it is important to be as clear as possible about oneself, one's prospective partner, and the nature of the relationship between the two. A thorough reflection on each partner's personal strengths and weaknesses and understandings of and expectations for marriage is very helpful. It is possible that one or both partners are unfit for the high calling of marriage. Each should make sure that their mutualities are of the firmer sort, grounded in solid friendship rather than fervent romantic longings, though those too have their place. Certainly the couple should be clear about the specific nature of Christian marriage. This whole exercise in clarity cannot be adequately carried off without the competent counseling of a Christian pastor or wise person. Again, the nurture and guidance of the Christian community is indispensable.

Expanded awareness is a second step. Those wishing to enter marriage as a Christian calling should be fully aware of centrifugal, often destructive, pressures they will meet in our modern world. They will be living in a world that celebrates an ethic of self-enhancement at the expense of marital sacrifice and compromise, that winks at infidelity, and whose practice of lifelong commitment is faulty, to say the least.

Moreover, they should be aware of the tendency of the modern world constantly to revise the Christian doctrine of marriage to make it less "restrictive" and "exclusive" and to make family life less time-consuming and disciplined. Hiding beneath these "liberating" impulses is a general enshrinement of self-enhancement as a dominant motif. Many moderns think "you can have it all." It is not true. Couples cannot have flourishing marriage and family life if they give in to the pressures of the imperial self. Such a capitulation only means conflict, strife, and eventual breakup.

Conversely, persons entering marriage should be aware of the help available to them. Churches as well as secular social agencies are directing their attention to the preservation of marriages. We seem to be waking up to the crucial significance of stable marriage and family life.

Third, once a couple is clear about themselves and the firmness of their mutualities, and aware of the threats and possibilities of the wider world, it is time to respond to their calling to married life by disciplined attachment. That is, they announce their willingness to commit themselves to a specifically Christian form of marriage. They respond to the call to be formed into the Christian vision of marriage.

This Christian form can be discussed under three rubrics—the context, time frame, and substance of the marriage vow. First, let us look at context. Far from being limited to a private vow between two persons, as our individualistic culture seems to maintain, Christian promise-making in marriage has many contexts, all of which are important. There is, of course, the interpersonal nature of the vow wherein each promises: "I take you to be my wife/husband from this day forward . . ." Even preceding that, however, is the *intra*personal nature of the promise. I promise *myself* that I take the other in faithfulness. Even before I make a promise to another, I agree to bind myself by that vow. Without that first step, promise-making does not make sense.

Beyond the intra- and interpersonal nature of marriage vows, the context broadens. Promises are made before family and friends, who witness its solemnity and vow to support the couple in their life together. Further, the vow is made in the context of the church—the pastor symbolizing that context. Vows are made to conform to this particular community's understanding of marriage. That understanding has been blessed by Jesus "who gladdened the wedding at Cana in Galilee."

Further, the state has an interest in assuring proper and stable marriage, so it gives the church the capacity to make the vows legally binding. Thus, the couple's promises are made and affirmed in the legal context of the state.

The context of the vows broadens even further when the couple commits themselves to a "holy estate." The divinely given structure of marriage provides a solid referent for the vows. The church's understanding simply reflects this prior structure. The structure is an order of creation and preservation. And grounding that order, as well as witnessing the vows, is God the Creator. Christians promise before God.

These ever-widening contexts bestow a powerful social quality on Christian marriage. It renders pale and insufficient current practices of "living together," which lack the seriousness of public vows. Christian promises reverberate far beyond the couple alone. They reestablish the couple within an ongoing community that finally claims divine sanction for its practice.

The time frame of Christian marriage vows embraces a past, present, and future. The institution of marriage, within which Christians commit themselves to one another, was created from the beginning by the Lord God, "who created our first parents and established them in marriage." This foundation extends throughout history to the present time, and provides the precedent which we reduplicate in our lives.

By vowing to enter this tradition in the present, a Christian couple makes a sharp break with their earlier lives by entering into this new covenant. Their lives are radically altered. Their vows indicate a powerful rite of passage. After this moment loyalties are rearranged, financial responsibilities change, a new home is founded, and the "two become as one." Traditionally, this moment of transition opens the way for sexual relations. This is properly so, for it marks the moment of public commitment and validation, and it is fitting that access to the most intimate of exchanges be given at that time. Just as priests do not baptize or marry, judges do not render decisions, and presidents do not take formal power until vows are made and validated, so new privileges—as well as responsibilities—come with the vows.

Religious and secular communities alike mark this important rite of passage with all sorts of celebrative customs and ceremonies. Bachelor parties, showers, new clothing, dinners, toasts, and dances are a few of the most obvious ways that this powerful change of status is affirmed. When this rite—with its attendant sharp change in privileges and responsibilities—wanes in importance, as it seems to be doing in the present day, it is a worrisome sign that the vows are also being taken more lightly.

Finally, marriage vows have a future dimension. There are solemn intentions toward a permanent bond. "I promise to be faithful to you until death parts us." We are to "find delight in each other and grow in holy love until life's end."

At the moment of marriage, the partners themselves as well as their mutualities are immature. The vows of permanence are assurances that the partners will give each other and their relationship the time to grow and flourish. They further recognize the intentions of God that what God puts together no one should ever put asunder.

This leads us to the substance of the vows. They are characterized by faithful love—fidelity. Fidelity in marriage is to be modeled after God's faithfulness to his people and Jesus' love for others. As such there is a powerful element of unconditionedness to it. Married love is to remain constant in the "joys and sorrows that all the years may bring." Fidelity includes commitment to the other's good, even amid the changes that each shall undergo. It includes the willingness to forgive and begin anew, so that the instabilities inevitable in all human relationships can be weathered. It means affirmation and acceptance of the partner as partner, no matter what the judgments of the world are with regard to life in the world. It obviously means fidelity in sexual matters so that the deepest intimacies are never violated by moving them outside the bond. It means the willingness to become dependent on the other—physically, emotionally, and spiritually. It means enduring partnership in the bearing and nurture of children and in a broader service to the world.

Faithful love is not without costs. Sacrifice is very much a part of marriage. Both partners sacrifice their eros-wanderings, the priority of friends and parents, perhaps parts of their careers, and certainly the radical self-determination that is so much extolled by our culture. But the cost is small compared to the benefits.

Life under the bond of faithful love is not all heavy and serious. Indeed, it is within the comfort and security of fidelity that spontaneities can flourish. Frontiers of sexual play can be explored. Personal quirks can become the occasion for delight. Recreative moments—having a holiday together, having a fine dinner out or in, enjoying sports together—can multiply under the canopy of faithful love. Moreover, the trust associated with faithful love allows a great deal of individual latitude to pursue interests not necessarily shared by the partner, so long as those interests do not threaten the bond.

These elements of Christian marriage—its context, time frame, and substance—are what Christians commit themselves to in disciplined attachment. They respond to the call of God to participate in a Christian way in a crucial place of responsibility—marriage and family life. Their Christian faith becomes concrete in precisely this calling.

The fourth phase of fitting one's own particularity with a specific sphere of God's ordering of creation is what we termed "disciplined detachment." That is a strange, but unfortunately necessary, category to employ in relation to marriage and family life. It refers to separation and divorce. As a last resort and as the lesser of evils, divorce can be justified. When mutualities have completely broken down and the interactions between partners become seriously destructive, the possibility of divorce looms. But even before such negativities develop, and certainly before any separation or divorce is contemplated, Christian partners are obligated to seek the best counseling and guidance available. One would hope that among those offering their services, Christian practitioners of excellence would be available.

At any rate, when all recourse has been exhausted and every effort has been made to restore the marriage to health, and there is still destructive disharmony, divorce becomes not only a possibility but a tragic necessity. But it is just that. Both partners must be fully aware of their participation in failure and fault. With sober repentance, the forgiveness and new beginning possible through God's grace in Christ can be theirs. Through that grace, new lives can arise out of sin and chaos. New beginnings can be made on the other side of disciplined detachment from a bad marriage.

LOVE

We have already said much about the role of agape love in Christian marriage. It permeates the whole of our understanding. Indeed, a good marriage and family life provide the most palpable experiences of human agape love in our historical existence. They are elementary republics of love.

As Christian character is nurtured toward agape love, certain important enrichments of marriage become possible. One is the element of unconditionedness that agape contributes. The mutualities of other kinds of human love—erotic, pragmatic, even those of friendship—are unstable because of our involvement in finitude and sin. Partners change with time, they unintentionally and intentionally violate each other and their relationship, and they have rough edges that never are completely ironed out and thereby become sources of discontent. Agape provides the capacities for steadfastness and reconciliation that can overcome the turbulence caused by the disruption of mutualities that are bound to occur. Agape disposes each partner to repent, initiate forgiveness, and work at building up the bond that simply cannot be free of problems.

Such unconditionedness, when operating mutually between two Christian partners, provides the most obvious, sustained reflection of divine love we have. In Christian marriage each partner can experience unconditional acceptance. From such a haven many tragedies can be borne, and much energy can be generated to contribute to the service of the world.

Another "enrichment" of agape love is its summons to universality. Because Christian marriage can be so good, it can also be the object of idolatry. Partners can hold so fast to each other and their families that they close their eyes and hearts to the rest of the world. Agape struggles against this closure. It insists that there are other beings in the world. All are beloved of God with the same kind of love we receive in Christ. Therefore, our own love cannot be limited to our spouse and family, the most likely recipients of that love. Families strong in love must share it with the world, usually through their efforts in other callings but sometimes directly in person-to-person service when occasions call for it.

It is important to reiterate that agape invites and receives the partner into *mutual* relations, not ones characterized by an unhealthy dependence. Such mutuality tends toward equality, not the kind of mathematical equality so dear to so many moderns, but a kind of complementarity to which each partner assents out of equal dignity and strength. There may be asymmetry between the partners in many roles and functions and yet they may enjoy a high degree of equality.

Finally, agape love summons Christians to a particular concern for the vulnerable. Again, families strong in love are particularly able to welcome the stranger, whether that stranger is a foreign student, a lonely neighbor, an orphan, a handicapped child, or even a "difficult" child of their own.

One strong family in my acquaintance had a severely handicapped child. After the inevitable pain of working through such an untoward happening, the young father told me: "We have come to the conclusion that if God wanted to choose just the right family for a child as wounded as Matthew, we are it! We can care for him."

Thus, as in other areas of life, Christian love serves to restore, enrich, broaden, and focus our ordinary earthly loves. It transforms the love inherent in an order of Creation into a more enduring and expansive form of being together.

HOPE

We argued in the preceding chapter that as we are made transparent by the Spirit to the intentions of God's love for the world, our flaws are also illuminated. The facts of our continuing separation from God and from our spouse and family are also made clear. The longed-for perfection in marriage and family life does not appear. Our sin and finitude show up in this most intimate place of responsibility. Indeed, for some Christians marriage has ended in divorce and for others it may be a burden for the rest of their lives. Even for those with the strongest marriages, the struggle with sin goes on.

The good news of hope is that our salvation is finally not dependent on our performance in marriage and family life. Our acceptance by God is dependent on his free grace in Christ, not our work. This is a source of firm hope for several reasons. First, we are freed from placing ultimate trust in a "successful" marriage and family life. This gives us the needed distance from both that prevents the wrong kinds of expectations of any kind of human connection. We need not frantically grasp at perfection and thereby fail to receive the blessings given with grateful hearts. Second, we are assured of the daily forgiveness by God that enables us to pick up our lives and live every day anew—amid our flawed marriages and families. That gives us the needed hope to continue. We can move into the future.

Particularly with regard to the ambiguities involved in raising children, we can hope in God's use of our frail efforts. So many Christian parents in this modern day feel they have been failures as parents. They worry that they have failed in transmitting their cherished values and traditions to their children. They are aware of the competition from television and peer culture for the loyalties of their children, and all too often think they have lost out.

There are often rational grounds for feeling this way. But parents must understand that they cannot take responsibility for their children after a certain point. After doing the best child-raising they can and after making clear their steadfast commitment to them, parents must hope in God's ongoing encounter with their children. The Lord will use the lives of those children as he sees fit, not as the parents see fit. Moreover, each child will at some time or other respond to the initiative of God. God has not abandoned those children, who are both their own persons and the products of their parents' care. Our hope for them resides in God's sovereign power, not ours.

Finally, because we know both our achievements and our failures in married life together, we hope for a time of completion. Our marriage vows include the supplication that we might "grow in holy love until life's end." Further, they express the hope that "the joy that begins now will be brought to perfection in the life to come," and that we "may at length celebrate with Christ the marriage feast which has no end."

There may be no giving and taking in marriage in heaven, but certainly those bonds of faithful love that have been shaped on earth as a sign of the kingdom will not be lost in the fulfillment of that kingdom. As with all approximations of the kingdom, the bonds of marriage and family life will be drawn toward perfection by the good power of God in God's time. All the fragile, flawed, and interrupted relations of earth will find their permanence and completion in heaven. In this we can hope.

So, we have faith, love, and hope. According to the measure we have been given by the Spirit, marriage and family life become transparent to God's presence and will. Shored up and supported by the Christian community in its various forms, they become a calling central to the Christian life.

RELATED ISSUES

There are many issues related to the general area of marriage and family life that deserve comment. Only a few of them can be dealt with at this point, however, and they can be examined only briefly. Each of them singly are the subjects of book-length studies. What we will aim at in the following reflections are judgments consistent with what we have developed above. It is more important to develop a clear vision of Christian marriage and to nurture persons into it than it is to reflect on departures from it. Nevertheless, there are issues that surround marriage and family life that deserve comment.

FIDELITY AND SEXUAL RELATIONS

It has been assumed, based on Christian tradition and biblical injunction, that sexual relations are affirmed only within the lifelong covenant of fidelity that we described above. Following from this positive note have been strong negative strictures against sexual relations outside of an already existing covenant (adultery) and before the covenant has been publicly made (fornication).

The Bible's affirmation and strictures remain the same, the church's perspective also, though with less clarity and conviction, while Christian practice of the church's ideals is invaded by the confusion that plagues the broader culture. Indeed, observation of our sex-drenched culture would lead an impartial visitor from another planet to think that premarital and extramarital sexual relations are the norm rather than exceptional practice. It is difficult to find more than a handful of television, film, or literary portrayals of exciting and happy marital sex. The only kind generally portrayed is outside the bond. Massive exposure to such depictions is bound to make some sort of impact on the perceptions of the young.

Therefore, it is important to give reasons for Christianity's continuing affirmation of marriage as the appropriate and exclusive place for sexual relations. These reasons should be construed as supporting arguments for biblical commands, which, according to our argument, are not simply arbitrary or irrational.

The claim that full sexual intercourse belongs exclusively within the public vows of marriage hinges strongly on the symbolic meaning of genital sexuality. In this case we mean to use "symbolic" in its technical sense, that is, that something is symbolic when it not only points to a reality other than itself but also participates in that reality. Sexual relations between male and female are powerfully symbolic.

They can symbolize and thus participate in many kinds of human exchange, among them exploitation, domination, and commercial transaction. Sex among humans always means something, unlike the simple natural functioning of animals. In the Christian view, sexual relations should symbolize—point to and participate in—intimacy, love, and the possibility of new life.

"Making love" expresses and reveals so much of the intimate character of the partners involved—physical, emotional, and spiritual. Because of the variety of intimate characteristics, it takes a long time to become fully compatible. "Making love," contrary to popular depictions, is an art form that takes a good deal of practice for two persons to do well.

Because of the rich features in intimate sexual exchange, it is a powerful bonding agent. As persons share such exchange, their connection to each other is strengthened. Conversely, because of the intimacy involved, vulnerability grows with the bonding. In sexual encounters, the same intimacy that draws together can also be the occasion for deep personal hurt—ridicule, rejection, repulsion. Further, because of the intimacy expressed and revealed, including its capacity for both bonding and hurting, sexual relations are appropriately deeply private. Their intimacy, as well as the meaning associated with it, is destroyed in the bright glare of public light.

Besides intimacy, sexual intercourse symbolizes love in its many forms. Erotic love, playful love, friendly love, and even agape love can be expressed mutually in the sexual encounter of two persons. The more stable forms of mutual love press toward permanent commitment, about which we will speak shortly.

Finally, sexual intercourse includes the possibility of new life—not always and not every time, but unpredictably and mysteriously, the possibility is there.

Given these three symbolized meanings of sexual encounter in the Christian view, the Christian church has affirmed their presence exclusively within the firm commitment of marriage vows. Intimacy, love, and children can flourish best within the strong bonds of a lifelong public covenant of fidelity. The steadfastness and unconditionedness of Christian love provide that strong bond.

Thus, when two persons publicly commit themselves in Christian marriage, they give with their pledge a special gift and a special claim. They give each other in sexual encounter something exceedingly special and scarce—exclusive access to their intimacy, love, and contribution toward new life. If such access were routine and plenteous, intimacy and love would quickly dissipate. The contribution to new life would become confused.

As each partner makes that gift, a mutual claim is made. Each gives to and expects the same specialness in their relationship. That is part of the promise. And the promise is public and social. As a rite of passage, the marriage rite is the appropriate time for the gifts and claims to be vowed, and, shortly thereafter, actualized. Premarital sexual relations, even with an intended marriage partner, renders premature and confused a transition that should be timely and clear.

The preceding reasons are basically positive arguments for keeping sex within marriage. There are also arguments from the facts of finitude and sin. Many arguments for a less restrictive or exclusive view of marriage proceed from unduly optimistic assessments of human nature.

Regarding finitude, we must recognize that our love is not unlimited. Indeed, our capacities for Christian love are frequently shockingly low. We have to work at being loving, sensitive, and responsive partners. Married persons who have a history of working together to become those kind of partners share something very precious and solid. We simply do not have the capacities to work out such a partnership with more than one person. Moreover, sexual adventures outside marriage run great risks. The most obvious ones are physical—the contraction of diseases running from the terminal to the simply irritating. But there are emotional ones too. Unexpected and damaging guilt is one possible outcome. Another is the danger of serious attachments emerging out of a liaison that was meant to be casual. Finally, there is the risk of pregnancy, which, even in this enlightened world of contraception, regularly surprises those who engage in sex outside marriage. Then an even more difficult decision awaits the partners. We remain creatures; we cannot predict and control what will in fact be communicated in sexual encounter.

Sin is another reality that provides grounds for a strong Christian view of marriage as a lifelong covenant of sexual fidelity. Our self-seeking tendencies create all sorts of rationalizations for engaging in sexual relations outside marriage. We cannot wait, we need new experience, we want adventure, we need reaffirmation of our attractiveness, our present marital relationship is not as rewarding as we deserve. If we act on these, we inevitably violate our own promises by diverting the special gift of intimate love to another outside the bond. At the same time we invade the bond of intimate love shared by the other set of partners, if they are married. In both cases sacred promises are broken.

The kind of married persons we as Christians wish to become is marked by sexual fidelity to those with whom we enter the marriage covenant. Premarital and extramarital sexual relations simply do not fit into that aim. Full Christian commitment to marriage as a Christian calling includes it.

PORNOGRAPHY AND PROSTITUTION

It clearly follows from what has been said that Christians ought to reject pornography and prostitution. Both entail putting intimacy for public sale. What ought to be private is made public, either on a page or before the eyes of a stranger. What ought to express love and intimacy, and the possibility of new life, is used for other purposes—the gaining of satisfaction through the purchase of sex, either actual or depicted.

Both are tawdry activities debasing those who participate. It is a sign of the decline of our contemporary civilization that both are so publicly available and acceptable. There will always be pornography and prostitution. Christians will be among the purchasers of both. But it is clear that they do not help Christians become what they ought to be.

EQUALITY, MARRIAGE, AND FAMILY LIFE

Church and society are experiencing fundamental changes in the definition and roles of women and men, changes brought forth by the five historical trends we analyzed earlier. Women have achieved a greater equality of status and opportunity in a number of areas of life. Many legal and cultural barriers have fallen, with more certain to follow.

As with all movements of liberation, various phases are discernible. First, there was the claim that women are just like men and ought to be treated that way. Second, there was the claim that women are radically different. That phase was often characterized by a bitter separatism. Finally, as the movement gained more widespread and mature acceptance, it became less bitter and more accommodating. Each phase has had recognizable impact on marriage and family life.

It is difficult to foresee where these changes will lead. What is clear is that Christians will have to sort through the possibilities and liabilities involved in such fundamental changes, just as their compatriots in the broader society. Only Christians will have their own criteria for judging those possibilities and liabilities.

For instance, they will ask of these changes: Which will contribute to and which will harm the practice of Christian marriage? Changes that increase the possibilities of enriched mutuality will be affirmed. More equality of status and opportunity may well support such mutuality. Changes that keep partners too long apart, that fracture their shared worlds, that multiply temptation unduly, that substitute conditional contracts for unconditional covenants, or that introduce too much chaos and hecticness into life together will be resisted. Humans really cannot have it all. Sacrifices must be made if marriages are to prosper.

The same kind of question must be raised about family life: Which changes will support and which will harm the careful nurture of children? Again, parents cannot have it all. Careers, living standards, and social mobility may have to be partially sacrificed for the sake of family nurture. Christians should not fall prey to the illusion that the nurture of children is less a priority than having a paying job, achieving a promotion, or acquiring a higher standard of living.

It is the primary obligation of parents who elect to have children to care for them adequately, not the obligation of the state, society, or church. In this time of shifting roles, the primary concern is not which parent takes this or that responsibility, but rather *that* the responsibility is taken. My hunch is that nurturing activities will continue to be asymmetrical, with the primary responsibility resting with the mother, but with a healthy encouragement of fuller participation by the father.

We should certainly not glorify single parenthood. That condition is always difficult and often tragic. But once it occurs, the parent and children involved should get as much support as Christians can give. Beyond that, the church needs to put effort into preventing the conditions that lead to breakups in the first place.

HOMOSEXUALITY

The Jewish and Christian traditions have been opposed to homosexual sexual relations, though not always in a rigorous or punitive fashion. Their prohibitions follow from their beliefs that there is a divinely created structure to sexual life. Women and men are meant to complement each other. They "fit" together physically, emotionally, and spiritually. Male and female God created them, and they are meant to be as one within the bonds of marriage. In other words, there is *form* to the creation. Moral sexual relations are appropriate to form. This consideration rejects sexual activities between adults and children and between family members as well as relations between persons of the same sex.

This negative posture remains intact among all major Jewish and Christian traditions, despite strong attacks on it from some secular authorities in medical, psychological, and social-scientific fields as well as from a number of Christian scholars and Christian homosexual groups. The gist of their attack contends that there really is no persisting, discernible sexual identity tied to the obvious differences in biological form. Traditional differences, they argue, are arbitrary cultural impositions that have proven to be highly relative, both from culture to culture and from person to person within a culture. Thus, they counsel that love between persons be the sole criterion governing sexual relations. The "appropriate to form" qualification should be dropped, at least as it pertains to homosexual relations. There is less interest in dropping the qualification with regard to incest and pedophilia, though it is difficult to see why those barriers should not also fall, given their argument.

Nevertheless, those responsible for Christian moral tradition are not convinced. Neither is this writer. The biblical position seems fairly clear and straightforward in spite of the efforts to relativize it through historical-critical studies. Church tradition is rather unequivocal. Human experience seems to suggest that sexual identity has deep rootage in persisting biological form. The tendency of cultures to differentiate clearly between male and female sexual identities indicates a continuing bias toward complementary sexual identities and roles.

There is little warrant, therefore, for abandoning the "appropriate to form" requirement, neither among Christians in general nor especially among the leadership of the church. This does not mean, however, that Christians cannot have a nuanced and compassionate approach to the issues concerning homosexuals. Without relaxing their affirmation of heterosexual sex within the marriage covenant, Christians can strongly insist that the gospel is addressed to all sinners. Homosexual sexual activity is not some specially heinous sin that cuts one off from God's grace. Consistent with this, inclusion within the church and its pastoral care should be insisted upon.

As with all sin, though, forgiveness follows repentance and leads to efforts to follow God's will insofar as it is discerned by the church. The church should continue to call those who are homosexual by orientation—derived from either biological or environmental factors—to a "heroic" response. That is, they should be called to practice sexual abstinence, sublimating their sexual energies into other pursuits. The church has long honored such "heroic" responses and should continue to do so.

It would be naive to argue that this can be the church's only response. In our present culture, some Christians who are homosexual by orientation will engage in sexual relations with members of their own sex. Given this fact of life, the church should discreetly support those who try to maintain the bonds of fidelity. Such behavior is certainly a lesser evil than the promiscuity practiced by part of the homosexual community. The church accepts many less-than-ideal arrangements among its members—divorced clergy, for example—and can certainly accept and affirm those homosexual Chris-

tians who take the difficult road of fidelity. This should be done with
all discretion and taste so that neither the normative tradition of the
church nor the persons involved are compromised.

Beyond that, Christians should support a broad range of civil rights
for homosexuals in most of our common life, though there may be
grounds for discrimination in some areas, for example, the military.
But in terms of its normative moral stance, the church should maintain its traditional values even while it is pastorally compassionate
and civilly tolerant.

ABORTION

The final issue that requires an all-too-brief address is one that has
elicited intense debate in church and society. Many Christians who
were generally positive toward the Supreme Court's decision of 1973
have been appalled by the flood of abortions that has ensued. Others
were opposed to its provisions from the beginning. Yet another group
believes that the Court was basically right, that its ruling has ensured
free choice for women who must face unwanted pregnancies.

What many thought was a settled issue has emphatically not
worked out that way. Perhaps it is a sign of continuing moral vitality
in our land that such an issue has become the focus of lively, if not
acrimonious, debate.

My view, consistent with the view of my church, has steered
something of a middle way between the absolutists on both sides,
one of which countenances abortions under nearly no circumstances
and the other under nearly any. The Evangelical Lutheran Church in
America has argued that a couple may responsibly seek abortion. But
it is very conservative regarding the circumstances under which that
abortion might be sought. They must be grave indeed—threat to the
mother's life and health, rape or incest, severe malformation of the
fetus. Abortions of convenience are definitely proscribed.

Since human life is taken, abortion is always a tragedy, but it may
in very circumscribed cases be a necessary one. The fetus always has
a serious claim to life, and that claim becomes greater as it develops
into a baby. At the stage of viability—now pushed back to earlier and
earlier stages because of new medical technologies—its claim is virtually noncontestable. But at earlier stages, particularly in the first eight

weeks of pregnancy, the claims of others, particularly the serious ones of the mother, can be weighed in relation to those of the fetus.

Such a weighing is always anguishing and tragic from a Christian point of view, particularly since the moral presumption is in favor of the claims of vulnerable new life. Because the burden of proof is on the decision for abortion, the practice ought to be exceedingly rare among Christians. Agape love calls for hospitality to the most vulnerable of "strangers."

In terms of public policy, it seems reasonable and consistent to work for a tightening of laws that would restrict our current abortion-on-demand arrangement. It would seem best to allow states to set conditions on access to abortion so that at least a serious case must be made by parties seeking it. Most other Western countries have such provisions.

If restrictions are imposed, however, both the state and particularly the church must stand ready to support mothers and babies who are affected by the restrictions. If Christians want to be consistently "pro-life" on this crucial issue, they must demonstrate their agape directly.

This most divisive issue calls for Christian understanding and forgiveness all around. Few Christians are either cavalier or callous about it. Those who are not deserve to be heard with respect and forbearance. We should not multiply the casualties in this already costly battle.

We have spent a good deal of space on Christian marriage and family life simply because that vocation is so central to Christian existence. It is there that the most direct occasions for the nurture of Christian faith, love, and hope are most evident. If they are not communicated there, they face great difficulty being communicated at all.

BIBLIOGRAPHY

For further study of Lutheran treatments of the issues:

Lazareth, William. *Luther on the Christian Home: An Application of the Social Ethics of the Reformation.* Philadelphia: Muhlenberg Press, 1960.

Lutheran Book of Worship (Marriage Rite). Minneapolis: Augsburg, 1978.

Lutheran Church in America Social Statement. *Sex, Marriage and Family Life.* 1972.

Thielicke, Helmut. *The Ethics of Sex.* Grand Rapids: Baker Book House, 1974.

On biblical and theological approaches to marriage:

Barth, Karl. *On Marriage.* Philadelphia: Fortress Press, 1968. (Reformed)

Dominian, Jack. *Marriage, Faith and Love.* New York: Crossroad, 1982. (Catholic)

Everett, William Johnson. *Blessed Be the Bond: Christian Perspectives on Marriage and the Family.* Philadelphia: Fortress Press, 1985. (Protestant)

Gustafson, James. *Ethics from a Theocentric Perspective.* Vol. 2, *Ethics and Theology* (Chap. 5). Chicago: University of Chicago Press, 1984. (Reformed)

Marcel, Gabriel. *Creative Fidelity.* New York: Crossroad, 1982. (Catholic)

Nelson, James. *Embodiment: An Approach to Sexuality and Christian Theology.* Minneapolis: Augsburg, 1979. (Liberal Protestant)

Piper, Otto A. *The Biblical View of Sex and Marriage.* New York: Charles Scribner's Sons, 1960.

On a theological approach to the family.

Anderson, Herbert. *The Family and Pastoral Care.* Philadelphia: Fortress Press, 1984.

Mehl, Roger. *Society and Love: Ethical Problems of Family Life.* Philadelphia: Westminster Press, 1964.

On marriage and family life in transition:

Erikson, Erik. *Insight and Responsibility.* New York: W. W. Norton, 1964.

Kammeyer, Kenneth, ed. *Confronting the Issues: Sex Roles, Marriage and the Family.* 2d ed. Boston: Allyn & Bacon, 1980.

Lasch, Christopher. *Haven in a Heartless World: The Family Besieged.* New York: Basic Books, 1977.

Skolnick, Arlene, and Jerome Skolnick. *The Family in Transition: Rethinking Marriage, Sexuality, Child Rearing, and Family Organization.* 5th ed. Boston: Little, Brown & Co., 1986.

On approaches to marriage enrichment:

Demarest, Don, et al. *Marriage Encounter: A Guide to Sharing.* New York: Carillon Books, 1977.

Roleder, George, ed. *Marriage Means Encounter.* 2d ed. Dubuque, Iowa: William C. Brown, 1979.

On abortion:

Batchelor, Edward C., Jr., ed. *Abortion: The Moral Issues.* New York: Pilgrim Press, 1982.

Burtchaell, James. *Rachel Weeping: The Case Against Abortion.* New York: Harper & Row, 1984.

On homosexuality:

Batchelor, Edward C., Jr., ed. *Homosexuality and Ethics.* Rev. ed. New York: Pilgrim Press, 1982.

Boswell, John. *Christianity, Social Tolerance and Homosexuality: Gay People in Western Europe from the Beginning of the Christian Era to the Fourteenth Century.* Chicago: University of Chicago Press, 1980.

McNeill, John. *The Church and the Homosexual.* Mission, Kans.: Sheed Andrews & McMeel, 1976; London: Darton, Longman & Todd, 1977.

8

Work

A second major place of responsibility for humankind is work. It is notoriously difficult to define precisely the meaning of work. Certainly the effort expended in the nurture of children is work, but we have already talked about such activity in the last chapter. What, then, should we propose? Our definition runs this way: work is the human activity of providing—either singly or in a coordinated system—goods or services for pay in the private or public sectors of the economy. Since our definition contains the "for pay" clause, it excludes unpaid efforts in the family, voluntary associations, and church. This, however, should not be terribly troublesome. The most important human activities and exchange are not "for pay." A parent's bedside care for a sick child, the provision of dinner for friends, the worship of God, marital love, the exercise of political and civil rights are not for pay or for sale. If they were, their intrinsic meaning would quickly disappear. It is only a crude economism that attaches, or tries to attach, a price tag to all activities. As we mentioned earlier, it is a crazy world that assigns more "value" and status to managers in a dog-food factory than to parents who engage in full-time caring for their children.

Nevertheless, work for pay in our society's economy is extremely important. Managing a dog-food factory is an honorable activity. It provides a needed good in a complex and developed economy such as ours. And it has several meanings and purposes.

Before we move to a discussion of the purposes of work for the subject (the worker), a few reflections on the economic system are in order. An economy is a system that coordinates the efforts of many workers to produce goods and services for public and private consumption. It must deal with three tasks: (1) determining what products and how much of them are to be produced; (2) shaping the way or manner in which they are produced; and (3) distributing both the product and the rewards involved in the production process. In American society those tasks are coordinated chiefly through the pricing system of competitive markets, though the government also plays an important role in affecting those tasks.

While there are certainly ways of getting those three tasks done other than by competitive markets, I have argued at length in another book *(The Ethic of Democratic Capitalism: A Moral Reassessment)* that market arrangements combined with political democracy are the best. To condense the argument very sharply, I propose the following assertions, knowing full well that they do not handle all the objections and questions they would appropriately raise.

A good economy—in my argument, a market economy—is adept at producing wealth. It harnesses the energy and creativity of millions of actors to produce wealth. If diffused widely, growing wealth raises the living standards of the vast majority of people. From this many good things follow—better health, education, life chances, social mobility, and support for noneconomic activities such as religious, family, and recreational life. In short, an economy that produces sufficient wealth frees its people from bondage to the struggle for subsistence and enables them to pursue richer and varied human ends.

Second, a good economy allows a decentralization of decision making in a society. It does not encourage concentrations of power. Market economies, when workably competitive, coordinate in an unconscious way the decisions of millions of economic actors without central control. The three economic tasks we mentioned above are performed without central control, that is, without heavy government direction. Thus, the economy of a great metropolis like Chicago, for example, runs quite well without local, state, or federal government having to make the lion's share of economic decisions.

This not only makes for a more economically efficient system than government-directed ones, it also frees the government from the need—and the danger—to be omnicompetent. Government can attend to a more limited set of issues. It then can itself remain limited, a condition which encourages liberty, democracy, and pluralism. It is not a coincidence that the flourishing of democracy has correlated strongly with the widespread use of market-economic arrangements.

Third, market-economic arrangements support other social values that we prize. One is economic liberty. While perhaps not quite as important as political liberty, economic liberty is part and parcel of liberty itself. Economic liberty means that we can freely elect where we want to work in the economy. Such freedom, of course, entails a risk. We can fail to respond to what the economy requires. But one cannot have such freedom in a risk-free environment. Total security would mean total control. On the consumption side, we can freely choose what products and services we prefer. We can live according to our own values.

Along with the individual liberty encouraged by market-economic systems, those systems foster social liberty or pluralism. Because persons can freely dispose of large amounts of discretionary income, they support a massive and diverse private sector. Schools, colleges, ethnic associations, churches, recreational groups, magazines, newspapers, and charity organizations, among many others, are supported by the voluntary contributions of persons. Such a varied array is connected with market freedoms.

Besides the value of freedom, market systems generally are capable of dispersing many opportunities for economic survival and advancement for individuals and groups. There are various entering points, income possibilities, and occasions for useful service. In short, the opportunities spewed out by dynamic economies allow millions of workers to better themselves. That has been the dream—and to a great extent the reality—of millions of immigrants to American shores.

Finally, market systems deal out rewards for contribution. What the market finds scarce in terms of goods and services is rewarded highly. Those who can supply what is relatively scarce are given high incomes. Those who in great numbers can supply goods and services that are not scarce are paid much more modestly. Neither what the market requires nor the pay it distributes should be mistaken for the voice of God. Nevertheless, the market provides a roughly democratic way of dealing out rewards for contribution. Without such a mechanism the government would have to take on a massive task.

This catalogue of market virtues should not lead anyone to believe that paradise has been achieved. Far from it. The economy does not always grow—recessions and depressions do occur. There are many who do not share in our great wealth and who therefore have less "worth" to their liberties. There are many who cannot grasp the opportunities that are offered. The economy is not always characterized by fair, effective competition. Sometimes sectors of it are dominated by monopolies. Then serious distortions and injustices are interjected into economic life. Moreover, the economy often registers desires that are base, ignoble, and harmful. Pornographic magazines flourish alongside those devoted to the education of children. Markets ferret out and respond to a myriad of human wants. The markets' lurid variety is confusing and depressing to many.

So, there is much room for improvement. Government and private citizens need to aim at correcting the flaws of our market economy. Nevertheless, it provides the economic context, a rather good one at that, for our work. It provides the places of responsibility for our working lives.

WORK AS A PLACE OF
RESPONSIBILITY

While Christians of good will and intelligence disagree sharply on the practical and moral assessment of capitalism as an economic system, they are more unified on the purposes of work. In our day at least, Christians perceive at least three purposes for work: (1) as a means of living, (2) as self-fulfillment, and (3) as contribution to the common good. Moreover, not only Christians but also persons of other religions as well as secular people find considerable consensus on these three purposes, though they certainly might rank them differently in importance.

As in preceding chapters, we will first aim at discerning the intention of the Creator in a particular place of responsibility. That intention, though not grasped with clarity or completeness, is accessible to human experience and reason. Indeed, both Western experience and reason are strongly conditioned by biblical and churchly notions of work. These notions have contributed to the various sanctions surrounding work, though these have undergone significant change in the dynamics of history. Obviously, they have not done away with the ambiguities surrounding work—it is often too little or too big in our lives.

In the midst of that very ambiguity, God's rescue mission in Christ calls forth Christian responses of faith, love, and hope that heal and restore our working lives. Those responses transform work into Christian calling and are used by God's Spirit to nudge the world closer to the divine intention.

WORK AS MEANS OF LIVING

One of the most obvious purposes of work is that it enables the worker to make a living. The pay that is earned for the contribution of a good or service should at least enable an adult working full time to subsist. That is minimal. As economies grow, workers should be able to provide for themselves and their families at higher levels so that they can lead more expansive lives. When a decent level of life cannot be sustained by full-time work, societies owe it to those citizens to supplement incomes enough to lift their lives to such a level.

When workers are able to make a comfortable living for themselves and their families, they enjoy the dignity that independence and self-reliance can bring. They are not burdens on others. Further, they are freed from the struggle to subsist and can devote themselves to other ends—education, recreation, friendship, and associational, religious, and political activity.

This purpose of work does not assume that work has intrinsic meaning. A worker on an assembly line, for instance, may not find the work interesting or meaningful. But it is useful and is therefore remunerated, sometimes handsomely. A living can be made. On the opposite end of the scale, persons with very high incomes sometimes engage in their work not because it is fulfilling for them but because the income enables them to do other things. A rather wealthy businessman in my acquaintance cares about his business only enough to make sure it prospers. He then is able to direct his high income toward political involvement, which is what really interests him.

The extreme attitude toward this purpose of work is illustrated by the phrase, "we only work to live." While sometimes realistic and appropriate, such an attitude is fraught with difficulties for both the worker and the work. The worker can easily run out of motivation because the activity does not have intrinsic rewards. Her or his work then often becomes spiritless drudgery. Life at work is simply burdensome. This can lead to poor work—services and products decline. For instance, it is easy to sense whether a waiter or waitress really cares about the quality of service or is involved in the job only for the pay. Nevertheless, work as a means of living is a necessary, even though insufficient, purpose.

WORK AS SELF-FULFILLMENT

If "we only work to live" represents one extreme attitude toward work, the assertion that "we only live to work" represents another. In the former too little is expected; in the latter too much. Rather than being completely dissociated attitudes, however, they may be connected. Only in cultures that make too much of work—it is touted as *the* path to self-fulfillment—can there be a deep sense of alienation when work does not measure up to expectations. If unduly high expectations are dashed, even minimal meaning disappears from work.

Extreme attitudes notwithstanding, one of the purposes of work is to find a measure of self-fulfillment. Some of that self-fulfillment may follow simply from responding vigorously to the deep-seated human impulse to work. It feels good to expend energy into a daunting task. Humans are meant to exert themselves. Beyond that, though, are the intrinsic rewards that come when work fits the inclinations, capacities, and interests of the worker. Some farmers love the creative interaction of the land, their labor, and growing things. Doctors are deeply satisfied by excellent involvement in the healing arts. Crafts persons express their creative skills in their products. Managers realize a measure of themselves as they coordinate the work of others in performing a common task. Construction workers delight in seeing the work of their hands take shape in a durable building. Teachers find joy when they are able to communicate knowledge, skills, and the art of thinking to a new generation. Indeed, as workers devote themselves to excellence in their work, part of their own fulfillment comes paradoxically from living up to the objective requirements of the work. Their satisfaction comes from "losing themselves" in work that they consider to have an integrity of its own. Poets, writers, and crafts persons often have this paradoxical attitude toward their work.

These examples point to the humanly fulfilling activity of pouring one's creative capacities into the world in the form of goods or services. That activity is, as Karl Marx so clearly pointed out, an authentically human enterprise.

Certainly other elements of self-fulfillment, though not so intrinsic to the practice of work itself, are the honor, status, and prestige that are often bestowed on work done well. Internal rewards are obviously crucial to self-fulfillment, but reinforcement by those external ones adds a great deal. While often correlated with increased income, they need not be, as in the instance of a professor being honored by colleagues for excellent teaching.

WORK AS CONTRIBUTION TO
THE COMMON GOOD

Neglected in the contemporary world's emphasis on either "working to live" or "living to work" is the third purpose for work, its contribution to the common good. Though yet evident, "working to serve" generally comes lower on the list when persons rank their reasons for working. Part of the reason why they do not view their work as service often has little to do with their motives. It has much more to do with the division of labor in a highly complex and impersonal economy. Many people's work is one little part—a cog—in a complex machine that does in fact contribute to the common good. But it is hard to see how one tiny segment of the process is an important service to others. Yet it is. Without conscientious workers the productive apparatus loses its vitality, and without that vitality, complex productive systems cannot deliver what they have so successfully in the past—a variety of quality goods and services at low prices.

The self-employed, those in the professions, and those in small-scale enterprises have an easier time seeing the social utility of their work. Many are very serious about this dimension of work, witness the numerous efforts to honor those who have served not only the enterprise, but through it the broader good.

We argued in chapter 4 that all our places of responsibility are sanctioned, dynamic, and ambiguous. Work is certainly no exception. With such a diverse and changing market economy such as ours, society has the ongoing task of encouraging work and discouraging idleness. To some extent it can perform those tasks by the external sanctions of the law, income incentives, and social pressure, but it is finally rather limited in generating the motivational vitality to get the work done. That generation is carried on by familial, ethnic, and religious traditions which dispose persons toward self-reliance, discipline, pride in work well done, and concern for service.

Likewise, the larger society must deal with the ambiguity surrounding work. Some work is too dangerous, too socially destructive, or too morally tainted to gain social acceptance. We do not legally permit bare-knuckle boxing, the sale of harmful drugs, or prostitution, though those activities no doubt go on. But these proscriptions operate within very broad parameters and the state has limited capacities to enforce them. As pluralism in our society increases, those parameters become even wider and, except for a few obviously harmful activities, the resolve to enforce proscriptions wanes.

Our society is currently in a great debate about what goods and services (abortion, pornography, homosexual bathhouses, soft drugs) fall clearly outside the pale of the common good. Christians will make important contributions to that debate. They will make their best contributions, however, when they gain more clarity about work as a Christian calling.

WORK AS A CHRISTIAN CALLING

Much of what was written in chapter 6 describing Christian calling in general is applicable to work. In fact, many of the allusions were directed to the world of work and it would be tiresome to repeat them here. Furthermore, the task of reflecting Christianly on human work is complicated by the variety of work in which persons are engaged. Fortunately, a large number of books on specific kinds of work are appearing. Books on medical ethics and business ethics come immediately to mind. But many other areas of work are now being treated in specialized studies.

One of the most important contributions of Christian faith to a proper sense of work as a Christian calling is a negative one. Christian faith in the justifying grace of God in Christ frees people *from* the terribly tempting need to justify themselves before God and their fellow humans by their work.

This temptation is so real and widespread that it is difficult to recognize. For many secular people, living up to the three purposes of work is all there is. If they cannot enjoy a high living standard made possible by their work, find self-fulfillment in it, or be confident they are achieving something worthwhile, all is lost. Christians can have an even tougher row to hoe. If they feel they cannot earn acceptance by God for performing their work well, they are open to even more self-negation than their secular compatriots.

It is not that work in its several dimensions is unimportant. Work is important; it is one of the reasons we are given life and breath. But it is terribly easy to make it too important. Ironically, those who focus on the self-fulfilling and service aspects of work are most likely to invest it with too much importance. If I do not become the kind of professor that God, my colleagues, and I myself expect me to become, I can easily lose my self-esteem and confidence before those courts of judgment. And the sad thing is that I will never win in those courts. Too much confusion, finitude, and sin are part of the game.

If we ourselves do not impose such expectations, the world often does. Business and professional people are frequently faced with demands from their work that effectively force them to "sell their souls" to their work. Such pressures can cost persons dearly in terms of personal equilibrium as well as in responsibility to other callings. Again, it is important to be reminded that the gospel frees us from fealty to the "principalities and powers."

Freedom from placing work in an idolatrous position means freedom for work as a penultimate good. For those whose work is on the absorbing and demanding side of the ledger, the promises of the gospel allow proper distance. For those whose work is on the routine and pedestrian side, the gospel frees persons from needing "significant" work as a way of earning their self-esteem before God. They are enabled to do what has to be done for the service of the neighbor in a matter-of-fact way. Workers in those positions are just as close to the grace of God in Christ as those engaged in "important" work.

In chapter 6 we emphasized that faith in God's special grace in Christ opens the eyes and hearts of the faithful to an additional level of meaning in our worldly existence. We are enabled to respond to the "giftedness" of work, for instance, and to see it as a bestowal of common grace, that which the Creator showers on the whole creation.

And so we are. Work becomes participation in God's ongoing care for the creation. As such it needs to be done well. The most banal and humble forms of human work can take on a kind of sacrality when viewed in this light. Luther insisted that a humble milkmaid does more for the kingdom than the monk in his cell. Obviously, something more was going on in that remark than the affirmation of humble work. Luther was criticizing a system that raised "spiritual" efforts to please God above humble service to the neighbor. In so doing he dignified the ministry of the laity.

The work of ordinary saints becomes transparent to the work of God to re-create and maintain his world. Even work as a means of living shares in that additional level of meaning. Work that is intrinsically satisfying is seen as the great gift it really is. Above all, work that provides direct or indirect service to the world takes on that deeper meaning. It is that third aspect of work that the Reformers saw as part of the "priesthood of all believers," wherein each Christian mediates the love of God to others. All useful work shares in this "holy secularity." Work becomes a Christian calling.

Blessed particularly are those who enjoy all three dimensions of work coming together in their efforts. To make a comfortable living, to find work fulfilling, to perform a useful service to others, and to see all of this as participation in the loving intentions of God lights up the soul. Even such a great gift needs to be handled carefully, however. It must be held in balance, often not a very easy one, with other callings given by God—marriage, family, citizenship, and church.

There is no simple answer to this question of balance. An important criterion, however, is the principle of indispensability. Those roles that *require* the active presence of a particular person—marriage, family, highly responsible positions at work—tend to take priority. Those roles in which one can easily be replaced have less priority. But in any case the yes or the no to competing claims is often made in agony. Decisions can be aided and pain mitigated by the good counsel of others, but real difficulties never completely disappear.

Earlier on we also argued that faith entails finding one's own unique role in a place of responsibility, in this case, work. That is, one seeks one's own particular call to work in the world. We suggested that clarity about oneself and awareness of the world are important steps in discerning one's call.

Clarity about oneself includes an honest appraisal of skills, talents, practical and moral strengths, what gives mature satisfaction, as well as an assessment of how one best serves others. Awareness of the world includes knowledge about what kinds of work are available and at what income. It includes also an inquiry into where one's services are really needed. As we mentioned earlier, one is called to the juncture of where one's "deep gladness" meets the world's "deep hunger."

While this discernment is certainly an individual task, it is also a corporate one. The wisdom and vision of the Christian community is crucial here, not only in terms of one's own self-assessment but even more with regard to the need of the world. This consultation may not mean an alteration of one's occupational objective, but it will point to dimensions of worldly need that will affect the exercise of any useful work in the world. The church's deep involvement in the alleviation of world hunger, for example, can open up possibilities of broader vision for those contemplating work in multinational firms.

In discerning one's calling in the world of work, one must realistically ask: What jobs are available? How much do they pay? Where will I live? What are their long-range possibilities? Will I like that kind of work? Will it mean real growth for me? Can I achieve something worthwhile? Can I do the job?

But Christians must ask additional questions that are not so popular these days: Where am I really needed? What can I do that best serves my neighbor? What does God want me to do? Each of these adds another dimension to the task of discerning one's calling. They

Combine w/ CP.9

w/o talents, experience, opportunity a recent college grad may be dep on parents for a long long time

cannot simply override the practical realism of the first questions, but they may focus the mind in directions that may precisely be those which the Spirit intends.

The time comes when one must decide about one's work. That involves "disciplined attachment" to enter that niche to which the Spirit points. Ideally a general direction is decided upon before college days so that formal education can be arranged as preparation for one's occupation. A good education, however, is always broader than occupational preparation. It has a wider humanizing function. Furthermore, it is often the case that young people wind up in different jobs than their college education prepared them for. That is an additional reason for acquiring a good general education. Liberal arts graduates often do well in the business world.

Beyond preparation for work, it is important to be intentional. To be specific about one's goals, to reflect about how one reaches them, and to act decisively all contribute to effectiveness in one's calling. Intentionality should not be exercised at the expense of due consideration for others nor in obliviousness to serendipitous factors in life. Opportunities that arise unexpectedly may be a new path opened by the Spirit.

An unanticipated benefit of the dynamism of the modern world is the implicit permission to leave one occupation and embark on a new one. Second and third careers are a real possibility for many persons. Christian interpretations of vocation are not incompatible with these new possibilities. Christian women particularly have found a new openness to shift the focus of their calling from child-nurture to work for pay after due care has been given to the former. This new openness has been shared by other men and women to begin new careers at midstream, as it were. Persons then are allowed to work out long-held visions that were subordinated earlier in their lives. The ordained ministry, for example, has been a prominent beneficiary of these vocational changes.

LOVE

Besides an additional level of meaning and the discernment of one's own specific call in the world of work, both of which are the work of faith, Christians have a special moral summons. Agape love exerts a creative pressure within the Christian calling of work.

a true job is better than no job: narcissism masked by "search for meaningful work"

waiting to find that job that fulfills their soul + pays well

Cousin Eddie in Xmas Vac holding out for mgmt.

One important effect of this creative pressure is a discriminatory one. If the positive pull of agape is to contribute to the other's good through one's work, agape at the same time presses the question: Does this work really contribute to the good of others? Agape can help to set the limits of permissible Christian work, though it must draw on additional criteria to establish those limits.

For example, there is a lively debate in the churches as to whether Christians ought to participate in the creation and deployment of nuclear weapons. Can the others' good ever be increased by one's involvement with such horrible weapons? Christian nuclear pacifists say no. But Christians who believe in a deterrence approach to nuclear issues argue that Christians can permissibly work on nuclear weapons because the balance of power created by them has both protected the right of self-defense and kept the peace.

We cannot reflect further on such an issue here. Suffice it to say that the vision of agape provokes such critical reflection on the nature of one's work. Questions concerning the neighbor's good can be raised about other occupations: working for a tobacco company, for *Playboy* magazine, for some multinational firms, or for the CIA. These questions are not different in principle than those that Christians have pondered for millennia. Early Christians wondered whether they could be in the money-lending business. Luther reflected about whether Christians could be soldiers or hangmen. These reflections turn on views of human nature and human relations that stipulate the neighbor's good. Christians in the present age must continue to debate those views in the light of love.

Let us assume that most occupations do not provoke such serious questions. Most are devoted to accepted notions of the social good to a greater or lesser degree, and Christians can generally agree with those notions. Then agape love becomes a principle of discrimination within a particular calling. It helps to judge actions that fall outside the pale of Christian behavior.

Another significant role that agape plays is in the stretching of one's working role. It calls one to wider possibilities. We know that each role has requirements that fit it into a larger process. Those requirements take into account human sin and finitude as well as the needed excellences of the work. They press the person toward a highly particularized responsibility—they tend toward closure.

Weapons manufacture,

While there is no doubt that persons feel tightly constrained by their role, they generally underestimate the room for expanding the scope of their responsibility. Not only are there real constraints, but the persons involved have a natural propensity to guard themselves and their interests. Business persons often claim they must necessarily do this or that—they have little room to maneuver in taking broader "social responsibility" into account. Conversely, outside critics generally overestimate the business community's room to maneuver. They think that a corporation can simply decide not to close a failing plant.

Agape as either motivation or ideal draws one away from myopic tendencies toward a wider responsibility. It summons to risk. But not foolish risk, the kind that seriously jeopardizes the future of the enterprise or one's role in it. Each Christian, hopefully supported by others, must find the fitting act somewhere between defensive closure and irresponsible openness.

Such a "fitting" act might mean the adventure of a new position at a new place in order to be of greater service. Most often, however, it will mean the expansion of one's horizons where one is. The doctor may be awakened to the challenge of those who fall outside the boundaries of adequate medical care. The business person may become more responsive to the claims of the community on business, thereby transforming business from a solely economic institution to a social one. The line worker may become more aware of the need for higher productivity and make helpful suggestions to improve it.

None of these examples will lead to automatic rewards. Indeed, they will often be met with resistance. The world is not always ready for reform. But reforms are made by those willing to risk, and Christians should be at the forefront of the willing. They should act on the discomfort that love creates.

Finally, agape calls one to be most sensitive to the vulnerable persons around one. It has a bias toward the lost, last, and least. Initially this means a sensitive set of antennae for the voices of pain. One must watch and listen. Then it means acting, not in a sentimental way that glosses over the realities of the situation, but in a way that extends human care in the most effective way possible. This aim of Christian love can be exercised in almost any situation. Even those jobs that are not humanly self-fulfilling nor rich in direct service to others nearly always have a "people dimension." One works with others. Among those others are opportunities for Christian love to be expressed. And in this cold world, such expressions are indeed welcome surprises.

As a Christian who works in college teaching as a calling, I find that the special moral summons of agape operates directly in my life. The lure toward expansion of responsibility figured strongly in the difficult decision to move from seminary to college teaching. It was not that seminary teaching was unfulfilling or of little service; on the contrary, it was an excellent place to exercise my calling. But I felt that I could do more for the service of others through teaching, administration, and influence at the church-related college to which I was invited than at the seminary in which I was so familiar. In other words, the college's "deep hunger" matched my "deep delight." The risk was taken and my responsibility expanded. The results are not yet fully in.

Once in the calling of teacher, agape also exerts creative pressure. My natural inclination as a teacher, along with institutional pressures themselves, is to delight in teaching those students who respond well to my teaching. This natural inclination leads to some ambiguous effects. I gravitate toward my "disciples." Special attention is given to them. Brilliant minds resonate with each other. But what about the others? What about the middle-range students who neither succeed nor fail dramatically? It is easy to neglect them, or at the most offer them a minimum of attention.

The lure of agape calls me to equal regard. Not just the students I like, but *all* students are to be the object of love. That lure will never completely overcome the bias to have favorites, but it does prevent a complacent resignation to favoritism. Further, if I am to exercise equal regard for all students, I am called to become an active participant in the policy formation of the college. I cannot rest content with my own little office and classroom. The call is to broader responsibility.

The summons to care for the vulnerable is also a powerful one, though it gives no simple directions for proper action. Every college contains persons—students, staff, faculty—who are "hurting." While one cannot seek to minister to all those hurting and yet carry on the calling of professor, one can begin with those near at hand. The students that are failing one's course come immediately to mind. One initiates conversation, attempts to find out what is wrong, gives special help to those who want to improve. In short, one is pastorally concerned. Such care does not mean a relaxation of standards. That damages oneself, the student, and the college. In fact, pastoral care may lead one to advise the student to leave college if the student is not willing or able to respond to the calling of a college student.

Others who are not students need such care. Strangely enough, those in positions of high authority are frequently isolated from persons whose affirmation really matters to them. The "vulnerable" may not always look that way, but there is a ministry with them also.

HOPE

One of the constancies of Christian self-examination is the realization that one falls far short of God's call for faith and love in the midst of one's work. In daily prayers and in the confession on Sunday one brings before God the failure to accept in faithful joy the work that is given, to live up to the promise that one's opportunities and talents imply, and to love in an expansive and pastorally sensitive manner. Such awareness without God's promise of forgiveness would lead to despair. But the good news of God in Christ is that daily forgiveness is ours. In spite of ourselves and on account of Christ we are unconditionally accepted. The Word renews our hope and we can go on, confident the slate is clean each morning.

Further, we can have confidence that our work, in spite of its ambiguity and obscurity, will be used by God for his purposes in the world. We do not need to be worldbeaters. We can offer our humble efforts up to the Lord with hope.

I certainly am grateful for this hope. When I survey my twenty years of teaching, I am powerfully aware of its insignificance in historical terms. Files of obsolete, yellowed classnotes, many forgotten articles, and several out-of-print books, the muddled memory of thousands of hours of lectures, discussions, and conversations with students seem to make up the negligible residue of a career over half-spent. Yet there are those students whose lives have been touched, those readers whose thoughts have been stimulated. That

is some ground for hope. But a far-greater one is the confidence that
God receives us and uses our work in ways that we cannot fathom.
As Dag Hammarskjöld has written:

> To obey the order when it is given
> Then He can use you—then, *perhaps,*
> He will use you
> And if He doesn't use you—what matter.
> In His hand every moment has its meaning
> Its greatness, its glory, its peace, its co-inherence.
> (*Markings* [New York: Alfred A. Knopf, 1964], 112)

Moreover, when I ponder the motivation and effects of my work,
especially the more controversial pieces having to do with economics
and politics, I am sometimes grateful for their relative obscurity! In
the great sweep of God's history they will be discarded or used as
God sees fit. They are imperfect offerings about which I can do little.
I can consign them to history with the hope that they are no longer
mine but God's.

All of this—my work, your work, the whole system of work—will
be taken up by God as he brings forth his future. Nothing good will
be lost. Nothing evil will finally persist. Our work will be trans-
figured by God's work, and the whole Creation will be brought to
fruition. That is our hope.

BIBLIOGRAPHY

For further study on the purposes and meaning of work:

Arendt, Hannah. *The Human Condition.* Garden City, N.Y.: Doubleday Anchor
Books, 1958.

Pastoral Letter on Catholic Social Teaching on the U.S. Economy and *On Human Work,*
both in *Justice in the Marketplace.* Edited by David Byers. Washington, D.C.:
U.S. Catholic Conference, 1985.

Richardson, Alan. *The Biblical Doctrine of Work.* London: SCM Press, 1952.

Terkel, Studs. *Working.* New York: Pantheon Books, 1974.

On economic systems:

Benne, Robert. *The Ethic of Democratic Capitalism: A Moral Reassessment.*
Philadelphia: Fortress Press, 1981.

Lindblom, Charles. *Politics and Markets: The World's Political-Economic Systems.*
New York: Basic Books, 1977.

Thurow, Lester. *The Zero-Sum Society: Distribution and the Possibilities for Economic Change.* New York: Basic Books, 1980.

Wogaman, Philip. *The Great Economic Debate: An Ethical Analysis.* Philadelphia: Westminster Press, 1977.

On the ministry of the laity in work:

Diehl, William E. *Thank God It's Monday.* Philadelphia: Fortress Press, 1982.

Gibbs, Mark. *Christians with Secular Power.* Philadelphia: Fortress Press, 1981.

Mouw, Richard. *Called to Holy Worldliness.* Philadelphia: Fortress Press, 1980.

Vos, Nelvin. *Seven Days a Week.* Philadelphia: Fortress Press, 1985.

On work in the professions:

Campbell, Dennis M. *Doctors, Lawyers, Ministers: Christian Ethics in Professional Practice.* Nashville: Abingdon Press, 1984.

Reeck, Darrell. *Ethics for the Professions: A Christian Perspective.* Minneapolis: Augsburg, 1982.

On medical ethics:

Beauchamp, Tom L., and James Childress. *Principles of Biomedical Ethics.* New York and Oxford: Oxford University Press, 1979.

Gustafson, James. *The Contributions of Theology to Medical Ethics.* Milwaukee: Marquette University Press, 1975.

Ramsey, Paul. *Ethics at the Edges of Life: Medical and Legal Intersections.* New Haven: Yale University Press, 1978.

On business ethics:

Williams, Oliver, and John Houck. *Full Value: Cases in Christian Business Ethics.* New York: Harper & Row, 1978.

9

Public Life

Render to Caesar the things that are Caesar's, and to God the things that
are God's.

(Luke 20:25)

We now turn to a third place of responsibility that can become a
Christian calling. We will call this third place "public life," by which
we will mean the spheres of both formal politics and voluntary
associations. Responsibility in both these spheres goes beyond the
privacy of family life. The family is too small a unit to perform the
public functions of politics and voluntary associations. Further, the
family's need for intimacy and unconditional acceptance renders it
inappropriate for those functions. Public life is also different from
work in that citizens do not get paid for their political and associational responsibilities. If they are paid legitimately, then their public
roles are their work, or at least part of their work. Many persons are
employed in government and by voluntary associations, of course,
but then their roles go beyond the common responsibilities of citizens. We will be examining the common responsibilities of citizens.

Before we can do that, however, we must delineate the purposes
of political and associational life. This is no easy task because there
is such a wide variety of political and social arrangements in the
world, and our own account of normative purposes will inevitably be
conditioned by the Western context in which we live. That context

174

has been characterized by economic, political, and cultural developments that have not been duplicated elsewhere. Therefore, our discussion of the ends of government and associations will be even more historically conditioned than that of marriage and family life and of work. But since there can be no simple recourse to an allegedly universal perspective on these matters, the fact of their historically relative character should not prove too debilitating. Among people of the developed West there is a rather strong consensus on the general principles we are about to elaborate.

Governments, in order to gain and maintain legitimacy, must effectively pursue four major purposes. They must aim at: (1) domestic and international security and order, (2) economic health, (3) the preservation and extension of justice, and (4) the promotion of humane values. Insofar as they are successful in achieving these aims they contribute to the common good of their people. Needless to say, governments alone cannot and should not purport to secure the whole common good. Voluntary associations, as well as families, are also important in that task.

Governments must first of all establish and protect a certain level of security and order among their people. Without those civilized life cannot go on. Laws must be enforced so that at least a minimum of secure order is preserved. Likewise, a nation must guarantee basic security from external threats. It must have a credible defense, or at least arrange alliances to that effect.

Proportional to their economic and political power, governments also take on responsibility in international affairs. Large powers are particularly responsible for a secure international order. That task is made more complex and difficult, however, by the further requirement that this order include a modicum of justice. Thus, governmental foreign policy must not only ensure basic security for its people, it must strive toward a peaceful and orderly world consonant with its vision of justice. It cannot rest easily with an order based on oppression, nor can it acquiesce to disorder as a permanent condition.

Second, governments must aim at a healthy economy. Normally that means an efficient and growing one. In our democratic capitalist arrangement, most economic functioning is left to private actors in a competitive market economy. But that allowance is itself a political decision. More governmental intervention in economic decision making is a viable political option, as parties of the left often commend to our Western societies.

Regardless of the degree of government intervention in economic decision making, other background tasks are important. The government must create an orderly legal framework in which economic activity can flourish, it must adopt wise monetary and fiscal policies, and it must intervene constructively when economic processes break down seriously. And, as the world grows more interdependent economically, government must aim at sound trade and aid policies.

Third, government must promote justice. Order, security, and economic well-being are important ends, but without considerations of justice they can be achieved just as well in a prison. What is justice? Relying on Western liberal developments of the notion, perhaps best systematized by John Rawls in his *Theory of Justice*, we can propose three basic principles. Justice is the fair distribution of liberty, fair equality of opportunity, and a social minimum for its citizens.

Liberty has both a public and a private dimension. Publicly, distribution of liberty means the right to run for political office and the right of consent. Each person has the right to equal participation in the process by which those who govern are selected. This means access to office and government by consent, that is, that holders of political authority are dependent on the votes of the electorate and must periodically be subject to a process that passes judgment on them. In this way persons are free to participate indirectly in shaping the laws that govern their lives.

Democratic government, then, carries within it a limitation upon arbitrary public power. It also provides—constitutionally—for private or "civil liberties." Freedom of speech, assembly, and religion; freedom of thought, of the right to hold property; and freedom from arbitrary arrest, seizure, and torture—all guaranteed by law—make up an array of rights that are to be distributed equally to all. These protect the right of people to live freely according to their own values, as long as that does not injure the liberty of others.

If equal public and private liberties constitute the first principle of justice, then fair equality of opportunity is a necessary second. It applies primarily to the productive slots in the private and public sectors of the economy. The "equality of opportunity" clause stipulates that those slots be filled by persons selected according to proper criteria. Improper criteria such as race, religion, and sex are ruled out. In short, positions are open to those who can best do the job.

The qualifier "fair" refers to the requirement that those who have serious social disadvantages receive special treatment intended to move them closer to the same starting line in the open competition to fill productive slots in society. Programs like Head Start illustrate such special treatment.

A third principle applies to those who cannot be expected to make their own way in the society and to those who, while able to work, are not currently self-supporting. The first group—the handicapped, the elderly, the incapacitated, the children of the poor—are entitled by this third principle of justice to a comfortable standard of living. Food, shelter, medical care, appropriate education, a decent amount of discretionary income, and dignified treatment ought to be guaranteed by law in an affluent society such as ours. As the general standard of living in the whole society rises, so should the prospects of this group.

The second category—the able-bodied who are not self-supporting—represent a more difficult problem. They are entitled to a level of support that assures a decent standard of living but yet is austere enough to provide a disincentive for remaining at that level. This minimal level should be accompanied by opportunities, perhaps even the requirement, for work and by educational services that will help them to acquire marketable skills.

(For a systematic and detailed examination of these principles, see John Rawl's *Theory of Justice,* or my interpretation of them in *The Ethic of Democratic Capitalism.*)

A fourth purpose of government is to foster humane values. The government is to support the shared values of the broader culture that make for harmonious and just civil life. This is a difficult task because of the growing pluralism of our society. It is also somewhat problematic because liberal political traditions such as ours generally leave the fulfillment of substantive values—those that stipulate the purposes or ends of human life—to private groups. The government is not viewed as the moral and spiritual teacher of the people. And this is properly so, since the government, with its great power, could quickly become tyrannical, if not totalitarian, were it charged with the complete formation of its people into the good life.

Nevertheless, the government ought not remain noncommital about those substantive values. Since it arises from and is legitimated by a broad Judeo-Christian culture, it ought to encourage stable family life, monogamous marriage, public decency, liberal education, the protection of fetal life, lively associational life, and religion.

It is notoriously difficult to be precise about what specifically should be promoted and what discouraged. But more and more we are finding that it is impossible for the government at various levels to remain neutral on matters like abortion or pornography, to list only two examples. Liberalism has its limits. Cultural chaos is as much a threat to the common good as cultural tyranny. So a middle ground must be sought that reflects the values of the broad mainstream of American life. Within that mainstream a lot of pluralism can be tolerated, but not everything goes. Government already reflects and reinforces mainstream culture by how its leadership models certain behavior, how it honors persons, and how it argues its policies.

Nevertheless, the major transmitter of substantive values is not government. Besides the family, the main vehicles for such transmission are voluntary associations—especially churches, private and parochial schools, and ethnic associations. In a less-organized form, neighborhood, ethnic, and regional cultures are powerful communicators of value orientations. Taken together, both formal associations and organic communities provide a good deal of the substantive values of American life. Government does not have to bear the major burden.

The transmission of basic values is not the only role of voluntary associations in our society. On the contrary, they contribute many things to the common good. For one thing, associations organized around a particular cause often act as the conscience of the broader society. Groups like Save the Children, Bread for the World, Friends of the Earth, Society for the Prevention of Cruelty to Animals, and Common Cause all raise issues of conscience for the society. As they press their causes, issues are discussed and often acted upon.

Other associations are purely service-oriented. The Red Cross, the PTA, and a myriad of support organizations for institutions like colleges, hospitals, and churches provide channels for voluntary service. Others are professional associations, often with a service dimension. Yet others are devoted to hobbies, recreation, sports, and education.

Indeed, one of the marks of our American society is the multiplicity of these voluntary associations, most of which make their small contribution. Taken together, however, they provide a good measure of common good, with the added advantages that they are self-governing and close to the people. As intermediate groups between government and the family, they are sources of identity as well as the vehicles for grass-roots action.

Taken together, government and voluntary associations pursue ends that are indispensable to the common good. They are arenas of public life in which persons can practice citizenship.

PUBLIC LIFE AS A PLACE
OF RESPONSIBILITY

A society is made up of a web of mutual responsibilities and claims, some of them formally ensconced in law and others informally embedded in convention. Government and voluntary associations have responsibilities to the people. In fact, a good deal of recent Western history is characterized by the expansion of obligations on the part of society to the people. More and more "rights" and "entitlements" have been enacted in pursuit of a wider justice. That process has had very praiseworthy dimensions to it.

But this process has not been without ambiguity. As persons have been encouraged to claim their rights a certain kind of dependency on the broader society has developed. Much has been made of the "welfare dependency" syndrome of the underclass in American society. While that is a serious problem for which no one seems to have any clear-cut solutions, a wider general problem is perhaps more threatening. That is the waning of the sense of responsibility *by* people *for* the society. In other words, we are experiencing a diminished sense of citizenship.

What is called for, perhaps, is a "supply side" approach to public life in America. Our political process has reflected the demands of a plethora of interest groups on the public weal. Not much attention has been given to what citizens ought to supply to their society.

There are at least four kinds of duties that persons owe their society if they are to be responsible citizens: (1) self-reliance and self-government, (2) civility, (3) informed participation in political life, and (4) willingness to serve. These duties stand in a reciprocal relation to the four basic responsibilities society has toward its citizens.

SELF-RELIANCE AND SELF-GOVERNMENT

Citizens owe to their society the effort to be as self-reliant as possible. This obviously means economic self-support. Not only does this foster self-respect among citizens but it also lessens already heavy demands on public outlays. If persons and families can do as much for themselves as possible, the government and voluntary agencies can better respond to the real needs of truly vulnerable persons. It may be important at this time of high demand for governmental services that persons, especially reasonably well off persons, not claim all their entitlements.

Self-government means that persons, family units, and intermediate groups handle their affairs independently as much as possible. A viable society is dependent on having a large number of agents who are not burdens or problems to others. When we produce large numbers of poor, very young single-parent families, as we are now doing, the cost of dependency becomes clear. But we need not point only to the poor. Our courts are overburdened with divorce cases that follow from the failure of self-government by married couples. Cases of juvenile delinquency indicate the family's failure at self-government. The breakdown of self-government at the grass roots not only adds to the public burden, it also brings regulation and intervention that diminish the liberties of people.

Of course, this is not to argue that persons refrain from claiming their rights and entitlements when they truly need them. But it is to caution against a too-easy acquiescence to the beckoning arms of the state.

CIVILITY

At the minimal level, the civility that befits citizenship means a respect for and observance of the laws. As we are able to participate in shaping the laws that govern us, so are we obligated to respect and obey them. Moreover, most laws have a moral basis that commands our respect. There have been and are instances when the law may be wrong and civil disobedience is appropriate, but such an approach is acceptable only after all recourse to change the law has been made, and then should be exercised in the most nonviolent manner available.

One only has to compare the New York subway with, say, that of Hamburg to appreciate the benefits of basic lawfulness. In New York graffiti is painted on every square inch of the car, many free riders wrangle their way on, no-smoking rules are disobeyed, debris is scattered all about, and the heavy presence of police rounds out the aura of lawlessness. Hamburgers ride in spotless cars, are "on their honor" that they paid, observe no-smoking rules, walk in clean corridors, and are happily uncomforted by the presence of police.

Civility means restraint. It means not moving quickly to the threat of litigation when plain human negotiation will suffice. It means taking one's place in line, waiting patiently for the traffic to clear, and generally not claiming more for the self than what one would allow to others. It means not foisting one's music on others, not disturbing public tranquility by boisterous, drunken, or profane behavior, and not violating the private space of others.

This sounds unduly fastidious, and I would not for a moment want to turn Americans into automatons. But what we have increasingly in our public spaces is a serious breakdown of civility. We will have to summon more courage among citizens to *insist* on civil behavior if our public places are to return to authentically common space. We will have to take the time and effort to directly call the uncivil to account.

Finally, civility means an active sense of civic friendship. It means active politeness and helpfulness to others who inhabit our common space. This does not mean going out of one's busy way to find persons who need help. That is unrealistic. But it does mean a readiness to respond helpfully when the situation arises.

INFORMED PARTICIPATION IN
POLITICAL LIFE

Citizenship means educated attention to the great issues that arise in public life. It means a concern for issues of order and security, both foreign and domestic. It includes reflection about economic policies and the "social issues" of our day. Above all, citizenship means a concern for justice. Each of the three principles of justice mentioned earlier are surrounded by a cluster of issues under spirited debate.

How should economic and political power be distinguished in our society so representative democracy can flourish? Is pornography protected by the right of free speech? Is affirmative action simply reverse discrimination? Are quotas a proper way to ensure minority representation? What vulnerable persons and groups are missed by our "social safety net"? Is our welfare system increasing poverty? How should it be improved?

The same sorts of issues arise in the world context. They need not be listed here. Suffice it to say that there are enough issues to keep any serious citizen busy. In fact, there are far too many to be reasonably informed about. Persons generally select a number according to their interests and pursue those. They develop general political philosophies that help guide their selection of issues and their basic posture toward them.

The development of a political philosophy—either well articulated or intuitive—enables citizens to be critical of their country and its foreign and domestic policies. Such critical faculties, arising from a basic loyalty, are the lifeblood of democratic political life. They are the stimulus for needed reform. Functioning democracies are always an open project, guided by the critical support of their citizens.

An important part of freedom is the permission to be free of political concern and participation. Many in our society avail themselves of such freedom, leading commentators to assess this as alienation, when in fact it may in many cases indicate satisfaction with their basic conditions of life. In any case, it is difficult to equate such a stance with good citizenship even if those in question are self-supporting and civil. Since democratic governance implies informed participation by all adult members of the society, and we assent to such an implication by accepting the benefits of such governance, we ought not make exceptions of ourselves with regard to participation.

At the very least we owe political life at all levels a reasonably informed vote. Beyond that we owe the willingness to discuss political issues with fellow citizens since that enhances the level of political awareness in our democracy. We may take the additional step of joining a political party and supporting it with our time, talents, or money. We may even opt to run for political office, though of course these final two levels need not be viewed as strict obligations.

WILLINGNESS TO SERVE

A final duty of citizenship is the willingness to serve our country. This may entail serving on a jury, serving on citizen panels or, in cases of national emergency, serving in the armed forces or civilian defense of the nation. In the future, citizenship may entail a year or so of service on the part of young persons in either military or community service. Such a development would be consistent with the strengthened notion of citizenship we are proposing here.

If formal service to the nation is as infrequent and debatable as it currently is, willingness to serve and support voluntary associations is less so. Certainly every citizen ought to be able to find some niche in the large numbers of associations where she or he can provide useful support. In view of the importance of these organizations in our public life, participation in them is crucial.

PUBLIC LIFE AS A
CHRISTIAN CALLING

We have thus far discussed public life in secular terms. This is appropriate, given the pluralism of Western societies. We cannot simply appeal to biblical or theological grounds to establish the purposes of the modern state, though it is clear that Western political traditions have been heavily conditioned by biblical and theological notions. According to the perspective developed in this book, it is necessary for Christians to be open to normative notions that come from our common human reason and experience. God has given all his creatures capacities to discern moral imperatives. Without claiming too much for these "natural" sources, we can accept the good and the right whatever their source, just as we have affirmed worldly sources of health in marriage and family life.

FAITH

Nevertheless, the issue of public life is not merely a secular matter. As we have consistently argued, the eyes of faith perceive a deeper dimension in each sector of created life. The first important Christian insight is that the state is a part of the created order, given us by God to seek order and justice. Without those qualities, God's purposes in other sectors of our existence would be frustrated. Both biblical and theological traditions affirm the state as an instrument of God, though that affirmation is qualified by further considerations.

While the state has authority, it is a derived and conditional authority. It follows that the state is subject to a frame of reference that transcends it. The state is judged by something beyond it—God's will.

For Christians, then, there is always the possibility of conscientious objection to the policies of the state, for when those policies conflict with the demands of God, we "must obey God rather than men." Such an option has been exercised frequently in history, and will continue to be exercised as long as there are authentic Christians around. The Thomas à Beckets, Dietrich Bonhoeffers, and Martin Luther King, Jrs., will continue to spring from Christian soil.

Thus, Christian faith affirms the state as a gift of God, but at the same time holds it accountable to God's dynamic law of creation. Moreover, Christian faith denies any salvific power in the policies of government. The state is to seek order and justice, but it can never save our souls before God. It has the task of seeking penultimate goods. It will be fortunate to achieve a modicum of justice in this turbulent world.

These seemingly negative contributions of Christian faith are exceedingly important at this time in history. The state, above all earthly centers of power, has the capacity to claim godly power. Since the rise of the nation-state as the central political unit, it has constantly been tempted to proclaim itself *the* center of value, demanding that ultimate loyalty be given to it by its citizens. The totalitarian states of our time—both communist and fascist—have made and enforced such proclamations in a pervasive way.

Consonant with these claims, such states in fact identify salvation with trust in and loyalty to their cause. Western liberal states, with their built-in critical capacities, are less prone to make such claims. But all modern nation-states, with their great power and majesty, are tempted to play God.

This propensity for politics to claim salvific significance is also present in liberation movements, some of them supported by liberation theology. The energy and will of God are then identified with the liberation movement, and salvation is equated with the political, economic, and cultural liberation that is pursued. Unfortunately, when such movements gain power, the sacred legitimation of their aims carries over into the programs of the new government. Given those dynamics, the oppressed of yesterday can easily become the oppressors of today and tomorrow. Perhaps the best example of such a course is South Africa, where the oppressed Afrikaners of the past have become the self-righteous oppressors of the present.

To all this we say that the nation is not God. It deals with penultimate, though extremely important, values of the common good. Its effects are always ambiguous, achieving relatively good or relatively bad outcomes. It is beholden to the Law of God, but no matter how well it strives after justice and peace, it cannot claim to be the salvation of God. That is wrought for us in the event of Christ. The state's responsibility relates to the order of creation, not redemption.

Having said this, however, we must quickly insist that the Christian faithful must make the important distinctions between relatively good and relatively bad governments and policies. Failure to do so leads to tacit endorsement of oppression and evil. Moreover, Christians are called to participation in the political processes that make for better governments and policies.

In our own case as Americans we can say first of all that America matters. As the most powerful nation in the world, its direction makes a great deal of difference to its own people and to the rest of the world. We can go further to say that America matters to God, just as all nations in their own way matter to God. Whether or not America stands for just peace in the world is of great import.

We can further say that America, along with many other Western nations, has been guided by the notions of governmental purpose that we outlined in the first part of this chapter. America, for better or worse, is the major bearer of the democratic project in the world. It embodies a commitment to constitutional democracy, civil liberty, fair equality of opportunity, social pluralism, a decent level of social security for all, and widely shared prosperity. In many ways it is a product of the five great historical forces we examined in the introduction. But in other ways it is the child of biblical notions about the dignity of each human being. Those notions, refracted through the prisms of the Enlightenment, have become the basic principles of guidance for Western democracies.

Thus, there is enough continuity between the Christian project and the democratic project to make the direction of America an object of great concern for Christians. We are therefore called to be citizens, to live up to the basic responsibilities of citizenship that we discussed earlier. But we see an added dimension. Our nation is a gift of God to us and to the world that must be critically nurtured toward the ends that God would have for it.

Beyond the basic requirements of citizenship that all Christians should bear with seriousness, some among us are called to public life in a more expansive way. Politics can become a vocation in a more specialized sense. Such a course depends on appropriate gifts and talents, a special zest for public life, and the necessities and/or opportunities of a particular time and place. Christians must assess their own propensity for such an expansive political calling. Certainly not all are called to such a role, but all Christians ought to honor those who do make such a choice and who carry out their calling with excellence. Further, all Christians should be aware of the difficulties of public life and the need of public officials for Christian affirmation of them as persons.

With regard to the life of associations, the Christian calling to them seems clearer. Not only do Christians see God's hand in the vast variety of voluntary associations, they can easily discern some place among them for the exercise of their talents and commitment. As a rule of thumb, Christians should have at least one association that they support in some significant way, be that in terms of money or direct participation. Most of us have links with far more than that. Indeed, the problem quickly becomes that of limiting the claims of so many good causes on one's time and money. But Christians are called to the places in associational life where their capacities can meet the world's need.

In our home we have struck something of a compromise. My professional role entails many meetings in organizations of the college and church as well as a host of opportunities to speak publicly in those settings. The substance of what I meet and speak about often has public, political implications. Some of the additional money I make in honoraria is passed on to associations and institutions that

our family supports—several colleges, the church, world hunger organizations, political candidates, the PTA, and other charities that
occasionally ask for contributions. But during any given week I have
my fill of meetings and occasions for public speech.

My wife, on the other hand, does not have many of these occasions
since her main occupation is in the home. Though I attend a number
of meetings of voluntary associations, she makes the main contribution of our family in that regard. She is the "volunteer" of our family
and we are proud of her. From a Christian point of view such service
is right in line with the call to love the neighbor. So, her involvement
in several PTAs, a hunger pantry, a hospice, a church home for the
elderly, and hospital visitation is part of our family's Christian calling. No doubt such a deployment of our respective time and talents
is not possible or desirable for every family, but in our case it works
well.

LOVE

We have repeatedly argued that the grace of God in Christ leads
through the Spirit to a reconciling faith in God. That enables, again
through the working of the Spirit, the eyes of faith to discern a deeper
level of meaning in our worldly pursuits and to find our niche within
them. Further, faith becomes active in love. The Christian life inevitably includes the practice of love. One of the major zones in which
Christian love is expressed is public life. We have just seen how, in
many charitable and service organizations, love can be directly expressed. But in many areas of public life love as both motivation and
ideal must be mediated through principles and structures that are not
direct expressions of love. They may be expressions of justice or of
civic responsibility, both of which entail involvement in the ambiguities of political partisanship and the exercise of power, perhaps
even coercion.

Thus, as love seeks justice in public life it involves itself in theories
of justice, political options, and practical judgments about which
Christians of good will can disagree. Christians are sharply divided
over American policy concerning Central America, nuclear power,
deterrence, capital punishment, and abortion, to name but a few. Yet
each of those policies are connected with considerations about justice
and the common good. Christians involved in debates about such

policies are trying to distribute their love through just-making policies. But in each case their love is expressed indirectly through generally ambiguous and therefore debatable principles and policies.

This should not surprise anyone. For as policies become more
specific they get caught up in the vortex of complexities and ambiguities that characterize our finite and sinful world. Who really knows
with certainty, for instance, what welfare policies will truly benefit
the poor? Or whether nuclear energy should be abolished? No one
can be absolutely certain about the answers to such questions, but
policies must nevertheless be framed and administered.

Yet, while there can be no certainty about politics, it is not the case
that "anything goes." There are criteria for judgment that are not
arbitrary. Adequate empirical facts, historical experience, principles
derived from secular philosophical sources, and the insights of social
sciences all enter into sound judgments. For Christians the insights
that come from biblical and theological sources are particularly important. As all of these factors come into play, Christians further ask
the question: Will this policy move with the call of love? Will it
exhibit concern for God's universe of Being and for the vulnerable?
In this way Christians use love as a norm for discriminating among
competing policies. While love can provide no conclusive, detailed
direction for policy making, it does embody a presumption or bias
that helps to sort things out. But its presumptions must interact with
all the other sources we have mentioned in order to come to a political
judgment. Thus, many Christians believe that a love that seeks justice leads to a policy of nuclear deterrence, in which the threat of
horrible weapons keeps the peace through a balance of terror. Others,
of course, strongly disagree.

Other issues are not quite so complex. Love leads Christians to
prefer policies that are nondiscriminatory in terms of race, for example. It disposes Christians to support policies that provide a better life
for the handicapped or that protect families threatened by cata-
strophic illness. The means by which such policies are executed may
require further debate, but the purposes of the policies gain fairly
unanimous consent.

The fact that public life is caught up in so much ambiguity demands two further qualities of agape love: its capacity to initiate
action on behalf of others and its capacity to forgive. The very ambi-

guity of politics often discourages people from venturing outside their private worlds. Combined with the private orientation of a hedonistic life style, the ambiguity of public life disposes too many persons to shun both political and associational life. It is this tendency that can be overcome by Christians who embody agape love. They will have enough commitment to those outside themselves and their families to initiate care for their public neighbors, in spite of the difficulties and ambiguities of politics.

The universalist impulse in agape love encourages political and associational involvement. It is the only way that Christians can love at a distance the neighbor who cannot be known or contacted personally. Such involvement is also a major way that Christians can address the plight of the poor, vulnerable, and defenseless. Political instruments and processes are crucial to arranging laws and structures that are beneficial to the poor and that go beyond the vagaries of charity. For example, laws that guarantee compensation for the unemployed are more just and reliable than making the unemployed dependent on the generosity of the better-off, who may or may not wish to donate their money for that purpose.

Christians should be quite aware that the just-making aims of love are controversial. Wise policy is difficult to shape, even though utterly necessary. Policies that are unduly "open"—in our continuum from closure to openness—can become permissive and sentimental. They can arrange incentives for the poor, for example, that actually increase their dependency and thereby diminish their dignity. On the other hand, policies that are unduly "closed" can become punitive and ungenerous. They can hurt or neglect large numbers of people and thereby exacerbate social conflicts.

In a thumbnail depiction, the first set of dangers falls to political liberals, the second to conservatives. The former is overly optimistic about human nature, the latter overly pessimistic. This divide is evident in political debates over domestic and foreign policy. Christians should have at their disposal enough wisdom about human nature to avoid dangerous extremes. Reinhold Niebuhr, who combined both reforming zeal and hardheaded realism, argued that a Christian interpretation of human nature respects both humanity's capacity for justice as well as its capacity for sin.

My own hunch is that the Christian quest for justice in these times will have to go beyond the conventional attitudes of traditional liberalism and conservatism. It will aim at forging justice in tightfisted times. This will mean that justice will have to be extended in ways that are more efficient and decentralized than at present. Such efforts will have to have proper regard for incentives and will have to be channeled through small-scale institutions that are close to the people being helped.

For example, one of the most important tasks in achieving a more just society is the extension of quality primary and secondary education to the poor, especially in our inner cities. Presently we have the ironic situation of inner-city Catholic schools having to close even when the parents of poor children are lining up to get their children into them. They know that Catholic schools can educate the poor in a context of discipline and moral direction. Yet they cannot afford the tuition and the church cannot afford to keep many of those schools open.

A just educational policy would find some way to support either the schools or the needy parents so that quality education could go on. The mechanism of support might be through direct institutional subsidy or through a modified voucher system that would be biased toward the poor. At any rate, making such education available to more poor children would be a blow for justice. At the same time it would be more efficient than relying exclusively on our ponderous public system, and would be decentralized into smaller schools more open to parental involvement.

Many Christians, as well as secular persons, would disagree strongly with what I have just written. They would think it too neo-liberal or neo-conservative. That is the nature of life in the public sphere. Persons of good will can and do disagree. As the stakes involved in particular policies are raised, the level of political division and acrimony also increases. That characteristic of political life lends credence to the saying that those who wish polite conversation must avoid discussion of religion and politics.

Public life can be a rough business, both for public officials and for participating citizens. Within nations it can bring friends to opposite sides of the barricades; between nations it can bring friends to opposite sides of a war. Christians are not immune to such divisions though one would hope that even in the midst of conflict a bond unites them that transcends all earthly partisanship. That bond is their faith in God's grace through Christ.

Following from that, Christian love leads to the capacity to forgive. The rancor of political life can be diminished by such forgiveness. It means an unwillingness to demonize the opponent and a willingness to distinguish between the political beliefs a person holds and the person herself or himself. Above all it means the disposition to forgive those whose commitments are inimical to one's own. This does not mean that one gives up one's commitments or struggles for them less vigorously. But it does mean an awareness that we all see things partially and often in a distorted way. Christian love means we can forgive others the frailties which we ourselves share.

HOPE

But let us not conclude this discussion of public life with such necessary qualifications. The nation-state is a positive source of identity for most people on the face of the earth. Governments have been the instrument by which peoples have achieved admirable gains in refining and extending justice. Associations are channels of human vigilance and care. Public life is a God-given place of responsibility for Christians to work out their calling for the common good.

There is no compelling reason why these achievements by governments and associations, particularly those of democratic regimes, should not go forward. We can look to the future with realistic hope for a more peaceable and just world. Christians above all should be able to contribute to such forward movement. They should be disposed to go beyond their own self-interest to seek the good of all. They should be able to "sin boldly," to act decisively and vigorously in spite of the ambiguities of their own activities as well as of those that inhere in politics itself. They should be able to do the small, necessary things that are so crucial to political and associational life, because the divine milieu in which they act transcends the world and thereby bestows meaning to acts which the world would shroud in obscurity. They should be able to act with the proper detachment from politics—not giving them idolatrous proportions—because their salvation is in Christ, not political achievement. Because they are free from misplaced hope in various schemes of political salvation, they are free to devote themselves to political change that can result in relatively better societies. By the same token, Christians have critical resources that can help keep any nation from becoming complacent.

The public life of America is a brawling mixture of paradoxes. Too many people do not share in widespread freedom and prosperity. A tenuous peace is based on a balance of terror. The future of the democratic project is based upon the uncertainties of democratic politics. The innovative edges of cultural change are often vulgar and ignoble. Highly conscious of ecological issues, our society nevertheless places great burdens on the natural environment. The most religious of Western societies, we are in certain ways the most secular.

The paradoxes can be multiplied. God will judge our nation harshly for our many betrayals of its promise. Yet there is hope. Not only secular hope in the prospects of a great nation, but Christian hope that a nation given so much opportunity and responsibility can be an instrument of God's creative and sustaining intentions. Those who live their public lives as a Christian calling are crucial in pursuing that end.

Even with this positive thrust, though, we must not equate the future of our nation with God's future. The coming kingdom of God, true to its political imagery, will be a great community of God's people that will transcend every nation. All of being will finally be gathered into God's future. Judgment there will be, but in the end God's kingdom of love will triumph.

BIBLIOGRAPHY

For further reading on government:

Benne, Robert. *The Ethic of Democratic Capitalism: A Moral Reassessment.* Philadelphia: Fortress Press, 1981.

Brandt, Richard. *Social Justice.* Englewood Cliffs, N.J.: Prentice-Hall, 1962.

Morgenthau, Hans. *The Purpose of American Politics.* New York: Alfred A. Knopf, 1961; reprinted, Washington, D.C.: University Press of America, 1983.

Niebuhr, Reinhold. *Reinhold Niebuhr on Politics.* Edited by H. R. Davis and R. C. Good. New York: Charles Scribner's Sons, 1960.

Nozick, Robert. *Anarchy, State and Utopia.* New York: Basic Books, 1974.

Rawls, John. *A Theory of Justice.* Cambridge: Harvard University Press, 1971.

Will, George. *Statecraft as Soulcraft: What Government Does.* New York: Simon & Schuster, 1983.

On voluntary associations:

Berger, Peter, and Richard Neuhaus. *To Empower People: The Role of Mediating Structures in Public Policy.* Washington, D.C.: American Enterprise Institute, 1977.

Robertson, D. B., ed. *Voluntary Associations: A Study of Groups in Free Societies. Essays in Honor of J. L. Adams.* Richmond: John Knox Press, 1966.

On citizenship:

Mead, Lawrence. *Beyond Entitlement: The Social Obligations of Citizenship.* New York: Free Press, 1985.

Will, George. *The Pursuit of Virtue, and Other Tory Notions.* New York: Simon & Schuster, 1983.

On Christian views of politics:

Coleman, John A. *An American Strategic Theology.* New York: Paulist Press, 1982.

Lehmann, Paul. *The Transfiguration of Politics.* New York: Harper & Row, 1975.

McCann, Dennis. *Christian Realism and Liberation Theology: Practical Theologies in Creative Conflict.* Maryknoll, N.Y.: Orbis Books, 1981.

Mouw, Richard. *Politics and the Biblical Drama.* Grand Rapids: Wm. B. Eerdmans, 1976; reprinted, Grand Rapids: Baker Book House, 1983.

Niebuhr, Reinhold. *An Interpretation of Christian Ethics.* New York: Harper & Row, 1979.

———. *Niebuhr on Politics.*

Petulla, Joseph. *Christian Political Theology: A Marxian Guide.* Maryknoll, N.Y.: Orbis Books, 1972.

Thielicke, Helmut. *Theological Ethics.* Vol. 2, *Politics.* Philadelphia: Fortress Press, 1969.

Yoder, John. *The Politics of Jesus.* Grand Rapids: Wm. B. Eerdmans, 1972.

10

The Church

And how are they to believe in him of whom they have never heard?
And how are they to hear without a preacher? And how can men preach
unless they are sent?

(Romans 10:14–15)

It is the purpose of the Lutheran Church in America to engage as many
persons as will share its confession of faith in a fellowship of worship,
learning, witness and service that the Word of God in Jesus Christ may
become effective in their lives together and individually including relationships with other Christian fellowships and with social institutions
at home and throughout the world.

(Statement of Mission of the Lutheran Church in America [1972])

As we begin our concluding chapter it is appropriate to recapitulate
our argument thus far. We began with an analysis of our contemporary situation in the developed, Western world that highlighted the
ambiguous effects of five great historical trends on our world. Along
with many positive effects, the workings of technical reason, historical reason, the liberal spirit, the ethic of self-enhancement, and secularization have contributed to a profound sense of confusion concerning our religious and moral bearings.

The spiritual and moral "capital" of the Judeo-Christian West has
undergone a serious depletion. The West's religious and moral guidance system has become problematic. Increasingly shorn of confi-

dence in an ultimate context that grounds life and morality in an objective reality outside itself, the West has turned to the self as the touchstone of meaning and morality. And the self, finite and sinful as it is, is a fragile vessel upon which to build a solid spiritual and moral edifice.

Nevertheless, God continues to call us to be his own and to do his will. God's work in Christ justifies and reconciles us to God. God nurtures us and sends us into the world through his Spirit. We are called by God to particular places of responsibility—marriage and family, work, public life, and church. Our cup of being, filled by his grace, is spilled into the world. The faith, love, and hope of Christian people transform those places of responsibility into Christian callings. An unstable and broken world is ordered and healed by those transformations, even though their impact is partial and fragmentary.

As we argued in chapter 1, religious communities are the bearers of the Christian vision. They are the earthern vessels through which God calls us. We must admit that the churches have not generally been up to the great task of transmitting the call of God. In the last three centuries they have been fighting a rear-guard action against powerful competitors in the task of providing formative visions for people in the West. (Incidentally, the story is different in some parts of the world—Africa, for instance—where Christianity is on the cutting edge of forming visions.) In recent decades the established mainstream churches of the West have experienced serious declines in membership and participation. The quality of leadership has suffered. Churches do not hold their young. In quiet desperation, the churches fasten onto trendy psychological and political nostrums to appeal to people. Their confidence in their own religious message has faded.

We should not overdo this negative picture. There are many signs of life and hope. One of the most important is that the churches, aware of their failures, are ready to fall on their knees and implore God for grace and guidance. In such a posture the churches may be more open to the renewing work of the Spirit.

Regardless of whether or not the preceding paragraphs provide an accurate picture of the condition of the churches, persons who are serious about the Christian life will exercise a crucial part of their

Christian calling in the church. Christians are not actively loyal to the church because it is popular, dominating, or even effectively excellent. On the contrary, they are loyal because God has chosen the church as the vessel of God's Word of grace. There really is no other bearer of the Word. If you care about the Word, you care about the church.

In a sermon I once gave at a seminary chapel service, I leveled a challenge at seminarians who were chronically complaining that chapel was boring and unfulfilling. It was, they said, doing nothing for them. Paraphrasing a famous line of John F. Kennedy, I charged them to: "Ask not what chapel can do for you, but rather what you can do for chapel." Exactly the same thing can be said about our participation in the church. We are called to contribute to the churches' mission so that the Word might be heard. Thus, the church is the fourth great arena of Christian responsibility.

The paragraph above encompasses only part of the story, however. While it is fine and good to remind people of their responsibility to and for the church, it is also important to be clear about what the church has indeed done for us. In our chapter on Christian nurture we emphasized how indispensable the church is as the vehicle by which the Word of grace addresses us and liberates us from sin, death, and the devil. The most precious aspect of who—or, better, whose—we are has come to us through the church.

Therefore, we must inquire as to what we are called to be and do with regard to the life of the church. What has been given us must be passed along to others.

The Christian life may be possible without involvement in the church. Dag Hammarskjöld, for example, not only kept his Christian identity anonymous, he also kept his distance from the church. Nevertheless, his early formation was in the Church of Sweden and he consistently drew on Christian writings for his own nurture. While we can accept that he may have had compelling reasons for his nonparticipation, we can also say that the church was impoverished by his reluctance to contribute to the ongoing life of a church whose message was so important for him. On the other hand, the publication of his *Markings* has contributed much to the spiritual life of Christians after his death.

THE CHURCH AS A PLACE
OF RESPONSIBILITY

As has been our practice, we could launch into an inquiry concerning the general characteristics of religious communities and institutions as they have been made evident to our reason and experience. We could recount in secular language the analysis of a book in the sociology of religion, for example, Peter Berger's excellent *Sacred Canopy*. That would be consistent with our contention that some of the intentions of God are available to our human experience and reason. After all, Luther placed the church as an order of creation, common to all human societies.

But such an approach would be too formal and general. It will be better to plunge directly into a substantive and specific delineation of the purposes of the Christian church. We can identify six major aims of the church: the ministry of Word and Sacrament; worship and study; Christian community; evangelism; service; and ecumenical concerns.

MINISTRY OF WORD AND SACRAMENT

This aim is placed first because it is *the* essential activity of the Christian church. Where the Word of God—as both Law and Gospel—is rightly preached and the sacraments, Baptism and Eucharist, are properly administered, there is the church. This ministry constitutes the flaming center of the church's mission; all else is response and implication that follow from this essential proclamatory action. Word and Sacrament are the most direct address and presence of God to us. We are called to be and nurtured as God's people through them.

Both Word and Sacrament are decisively filled with christological content. The saving grace of God in Christ is mediated through them. They come to us from outside ourselves—we hear the Word and participate in the sacraments. They constitute our only trustworthy connection with the Lord God of hosts. That is not because we have constructed them godward, as it were, but because God has chosen them and established them as God's address to and presence with us.

When all other religious activities fail or are prohibited, as they are in some oppressive societies, this activity remains as the defining characteristic of the church. If Word and Sacrament continue there is the church and the call of God.

WORSHIP AND STUDY

Directly following upon the actions of Word and Sacrament are the inevitable responses of worship and study. As the church prays for the help of the Holy Spirit in assuring that the Word is rightly preached and the sacraments properly administered, so it also calls upon the Spirit to quicken our worshipful response. Confession, praise, and prayer are lifted up by the people of God in response to what God has done and is doing in our lives. Worship is the expressive response of our spirits to the prompting of the Spirit in us.

Further, the church's response to the Word of God includes a quest for further understanding. Faith seeks understanding. Therefore, the church provides for biblical and theological study for all the people of God. It realizes that each new generation of Christians must be taught the essentials of Christian faith and life. Sunday school, Bible school, Christian day schools, adult forums and classes are some of the means through which the church teaches the story. The church imprints the story on its people.

Moreover, because the church must do everything possible to assure proper preaching and teaching, theological seminaries are instituted. They not only educate and train the ordained clergy of the church so that the ministry of Word and Sacrament goes on effectively, they also engage in creative biblical and theological study so that the Word is interpreted and applied anew for each succeeding generation.

In an age of exploding knowledge, it is a crucial need of the church to educate its clergy and laity well. The laity's advance in Christian understanding should be at least commensurate with their secular learning and training. In order for laity to be taught well, clergy must be solidly grounded in biblical and theological understanding.

CHRISTIAN COMMUNITY

While the church gathers to hear the Word, receive the sacraments, worship God, and study his Word, it also comes together to express the community that Christian existence entails. Christian being issues in care for the brothers and sisters. That means bearing each others' burdens, being actively helpful to those members of the community in need.

Christian community also means support for persons in their worldly callings. It has become increasingly evident that many lay people find support groups aimed at bridging the gap between Sunday and Monday very helpful. Christians gather to discern and strengthen their ministries as members of families, as workers, and in public life.

Christian community is a major context for the formation of Christian character. It is in the community that the Christian story is practiced and embodied. The virtues of faith, love, and hope are expressed by mature Christians and "caught" by the not-yet-formed.

Finally, Christian community expresses the lively joy of being Christian together. It may not always have a heavy agenda. The homely solidarity of church picnics and dinners, as well as the celebrations of weddings and births, are reminders of the fundamental bonds that Christians share in the faith.

EVANGELISM

We have noted how the Christian life is marked by nurture (filling the cup) and responsibility (spilling it for the sake of the world). There is a rhythm between being and doing. The same is true in the life of the church. The three purposes of the church we have discussed—the ministry of Word and Sacrament, worship and study, and Christian community—are all oriented toward the nurture of Christians. But the life of the church, like the life of individual Christians, will stagnate if it does not have an outward thrust. The body of Christ must not only be nourished, it must be committed to the race. Building up the body is narcissistic unless it is exercised for the sake of others. In other words, the church has a mission.

An essential part of that mission is evangelism. Based on the Great Commission of Jesus in which he commanded his followers to go into all the world to baptize all persons in the name of the triune God, the church has always sought to witness to others concerning the Truth it has been given. Live churches recruit new participants to that Truth. They have known that the precious gift must be shared.

Evangelism is carried out in both domestic and world contexts. It is an exciting fact that many younger churches in Asia and Africa are growing fast. Established in the great missionary movement of the nineteenth century, these churches are now responsible for their own life and mission. Often their efforts in evangelism put ours to shame. For we are now aware that the "Christian" countries of the West are that in name only. Most of the populations of the European countries are virtually unchurched. North America fares somewhat better, but one wonders how long that will last in view of the fact that church growth has barely kept up with population growth. Recognizing that fact, the churches are rightly concerned about evangelism at all levels of their life.

SERVICE

If the main message of the church is that God has demonstrated his love for us in Christ, then that love must be reflected in the life of the church as well as in the lives of individual Christians. Christians, both individually and corporately, lack credibility if they announce God's love for sinners but cannot muster any love on their part for those same sinners. So, the living faith of the church becomes active in love for the world. The church inevitably has a social mission.

The church's service to the world—its social mission—can be discussed under two main rubrics: social care and social action.

Social care has to do with charity toward those who have been wounded in the travail of the world. The church has long been a vehicle of mercy for the lost, last, and least. The direct connection between God's love for us and our love for the vulnerable has been powerfully demonstrated in the history of the church. Care for the poor, the sick, and the orphaned, homes for the elderly and handicapped, food for the hungry, and shelter for the homeless have long been part of the church's service to the world. Recently new dimensions of service have been added—counseling, therapy, day care, homes for difficult children, housing for the poor and elderly, hospices for the dying, and homes for unwed mothers.

This service is a manifestation of the church's call to be hospitable to the stranger and sojourner, and to show mercy to the vulnerable. While most of this service goes on in rather undramatic ways, we do have occasions of radical witness. Mother Teresa of Calcutta, in her commitment to the most pitiful cases of human suffering imaginable, is in a long tradition of such radical demonstrations of Christian care.

The church has long recognized, however, that simply binding up the wounds of the world, while necessary from a Christian perspective, is not sufficient. The church must also be concerned about the policies and practices of societies that create the wounds in the first place. This concern follows not only from practical considerations but also from the theological ones. The church is entrusted with proclaiming the whole Word of God—the Law as well as the Gospel. God's Law demands justice, and if the church is really to serve the world it must become active in the quest for a more just society. It must engage in social action.

It can be involved in several important ways. The first way is what we can call "indirect and unintentional influence." This is the least controversial way that the church makes an impact on worldly structures, but it may be the most pervasive and effective. When the church is really the church, it forms the outlook and character of its people. As the laity move into their worldly callings, their Christian formation affects their responsible life in the world. The Christian person is called to act Christianly, wherever he or she may be. Christian executives and politicians, for example, can exercise their Christian convictions in business and government. Thus, when the church forms Christian persons, it influences worldly structures in indirect and unintentional ways.

A second way that the church affects the structures of society is through "indirect and intentional influence." Again, it works indirectly through its laity. But it is intentional concerning constructive social change. It may encourage discussion of social issues within the church, bringing the social teachings of the church to bear on the social challenges of the day.

It may, like the Evangelical Academies of Germany, bring members of professions together to discuss how Christians might better exercise their responsibilities. Those same academies also play a mediating role, bringing persons from opposing perspectives and interests—managers and workers, for example—together in a context of fair moral discourse so that they might strike helpful compromise.

Or, the church may encourage and support legislative networks that alert Christians to important pieces of legislation at local, state, or national levels. In all of these examples, though, the church is basically forming the conscience of its members. The church as institution is not a direct actor. In fact, it need not take a specific position on policy matters.

Many Christians believe that these first two ways must be supplemented by more direct forms of churchly action. Thus, the church has become involved in "high-profile," more controversial ways of moving society toward more just arrangements. A third form of social action can be called "direct and intentional influence." Here the church as an institution aims at influencing matters of policy. Good examples of this approach are the social staements of the various churches. By far the most important have been those of the Conference of American Catholic Bishops, which has developed pastoral letters on peace and on the U.S. economy. These letters have lifted up the moral issues in nuclear and economic policies that are often covered over by technical concerns. They have created much discussion—both critical and appreciative. There is little doubt that the church has a responsibility to make such statements. But it should do so carefully, sparingly, and competently. Then its voice will be taken seriously, as indeed the voice of the bishops has.

Another example of direct influence is the "modeling" role of the church. In this approach the church, on the basis of its own religious and moral outlook, anticipates impending social issues and arranges its own life or constructs its own models to deal with those issues. For example, the evils of racial segregation were recognized by some churches before the general society. Those churches opened their doors to blacks and modeled interracial community for the broader society. Similarly, some churches presently are exploring how ethical criteria can be involved in making investment decisions. These efforts, while particularly pertinent to debates over investment in South Africa, are also relevant to decisions on the domestic economy.

This kind of direct influence was called "social pioneering" by H. Richard Niebuhr. He thought it was the most persuasive witness the church could make in its efforts toward a more just society. Instead of preaching to the rest of society, the church made serious efforts to bring its own life into harmony with its own vision of justice. This struggle for integrity, Niebuhr believed, is not only intrinsically appropriate for the church, it is also more effective than pronouncements in convincing the rest of society to take its witness seriously. Society would be open to its own creative reform were it presented with just and effective models constructed by the church.

A fourth and final mode of social action is highly controversial and risky. But at some rare moments it is necessary. That mode is what can be termed "direct action." It is direct in the sense that the church as institution is involved. It is action in that it goes beyond influence (persuasion) by exercising power. That means that it commits its economic and political strength to get decision makers to do what the church intends, whether or not those decision makers agree with the churches' intentions.

Historically, the Roman Catholic Church has involved itself in direct action, sometimes, as in the Crusades, even utilizing military power. Such use of power prompted the Reformers to criticize the church's direct involvement in secular affairs. To a great extent the Reformers were right—economic and political control are not part of the church's calling. The church's role is to preach the Word of God and form a people in accordance with that Word.

Direct action is "high profile" and "high risk." It commits the church to particular policies about which Christians can sharply disagree. When the Roman Catholic Church directly supported political parties, it alienated some of its own laity, not to speak of other Christians, who disagreed with the agenda of those parties. Furthermore, direct action identifies the church too closely with partisan politics, when it should transcend and criticize all political programs. The church can all too easily be co-opted by secular power for its own purposes.

In spite of all these hazards, there are times and places for direct action. Perhaps, as in the case of the Philippine church's support of the Corazon Aquino quest for victory over Ferdinand Marcos, the issues are compellingly clear and the failure to act would be a capitulation to obvious injustice. Perhaps, as in the example of the Polish church's support of Solidarity, the church is the only institution with enough influence and power to resist the state's efforts at total domination. Perhaps, as in the case of churches' direct involvement in community organizations in poor sections of American cities, the churches are the only institutions left with enough financial and leadership capabilities to represent poor people. All of these are instances where direct action may be warranted. But even these involve real pitfalls to church and society. They should be chosen only as a last resort and for the short term.

These four ways in which the church affects society are part of the church's service to the world. Combined with social care, they constitute an important aspect of the church's responsibility in the world. That responsibility, it should be noted, will not always be greeted with open arms by the world. But that is as it should be. The church bears a vision that should outrun every achievement of the social order. It contributes most when it acts out of that vision, with regard to both its own life and society's.

ECUMENICAL CONCERNS

Since the Reformation of the sixteenth century, the life of the Western churches has been characterized by fragmentation and proliferation. Much of this was a tragic necessity in response to a church that had become corrupt, ineffective, and mistaken. Indeed, even today the variety in the churches' expression provides an openness to the Spirit's propensity to blow where it wills.

But the negative effects of this loss of unity have taken their toll. The church's evangelism has been diminished by competition and a cacophony of claims. Its social service has been weakened by duplication. Its effects on the world have been wasted by the impotence that results from disunity. This has taken place in an evolving context where great challenges have arisen for the church. The five great historical trends that were discussed in the first chapter manifest a challenge of the first magnitude.

The church has to get its house in order. After five centuries many of the theological and practical disagreements that separated the churches are no longer relevant. Indeed, many important strides toward agreement have been made. The recent Peru statement under the auspices of the Faith and Order Commission of the World Council of Churches is a case in point. In its affirmation on baptism, eucharist, and ministry, most of the world's Christian communities exhibited an impressive unity.

While we cannot and ought not expect full theological agreement or organizational union in the near future, the ecumenical movement of our time can result in more fellowship, cooperation, and common witness. A growing majority among the churches recognizes the importance of such gains and is committing itself to them over the long haul. The church aims at fulfilling the Lord's prayer that all should be one.

THE CHURCH AS A
CHRISTIAN CALLING

The church through which we received the call of God is also an occasion for the calling of the Christian. Even as faith, love, and hope are nurtured by the church, those virtues of the Christian life become active *in* and *through* the church.

It is important to note at the outset that the faith, love, and hope that are expressed in our calling to the life of the church are a response to the grace of God in Christ. Saving faith is first of all in what God has done for us in Christ. That primal reception of grace, however, has repercussions. Like a rock thrown into a quiet pond, it creates waves that wash out concentrically from the point of impact.

FAITH

One of the effects of growing faith is the capacity to discern a deeper dimension in the structures and processes of life around us. This applies also to the church. On the face of it, nothing could seem more obvious. Yet, such a response is not so obvious. The church has many worldly characteristics that, at least to the critical eye, seem to obliterate the transcendent purposes that it claims.

Viewed historically, the church often appears more beholden to kingly crowns than to the cross of Christ. It has followed political fault lines and engaged in internecine warfare on the basis of those lines, giving the lie to claims of a more fundamental unity in the faith. Sociologically, the church appears to sanctify the narrow aspirations of nation, race, class, and ethnic group. Psychologically, it comforts the comfortable and quenches the rebellious anger of the afflicted. By and large, it bores the young and offends the educated. If you do not go in for archaic social ornaments, the church seems beside the point.

Yet, at the same time, the church is the keeper of the story, the sacrament of humanity, the servant of the world, the body of Christ, the herald of good news, and the community of Christian character.

These contrasting views of the church accentuate its paradoxical character. Indeed, the church is a *very* earthen vessel. But it bears a treasure. Faith discerns that treasure. It lives in trust that God has established the church and uses it to make clear his intentions, communicate his grace, and gather his people. Among all the callings of the Christian, the church is a very special one because it conveys our fundamental identity, as well as provides the rationale for all other callings. While the church and its activities do not take up a major portion of our lives, they supply the comprehensive vision out of which the totality of our lives is lived.

Beneath the worldly characteristics of the church, the eyes of faith discern that it is one, holy, catholic, and apostolic. It is *one* not because it finds its unity in those worldly characteristics, but rather in the source to which all its authentic elements point, Jesus Christ. It is *holy* not because it possesses purity and righteousness, but because God has elected it for his saving purposes and because of the call God has given it to follow his way. It is *catholic* not because it presently exhibits universality, but because it strives to impart the fullness of God's revelation and to embrace all Christians through all time and space. It is *apostolic* not because we have direct access to the eyewitnesses of the events of Christ, but because we believe that the Spirit has assured an accurate continuity through the ages in the church's witness to Christ.

Certainly those churches that are most open to the Spirit's movement toward oneness, holiness, catholicity, and apostolicity are the ones most likely to bear God's treasure. Faith is not gullible with regard to the claims made by so many religious bodies. The marks of the church we have just mentioned provide clues to its authenticity. Above all, however, stands this criterion: the church must bear clear witness to the good news that God has offered his free grace in Christ to all who will in faith receive it. Where that gospel is brought to humankind there is the church, for which Christians can only be grateful.

If the eyes of faith discern that, in spite of all, the church carries the main clues to God's intentions in the world, they also aim at perceiving their particular calling in the church. To what sort of responsibilities in the church is each Christian called? We must first respond to that question by affirming a variety of callings. As Saint Paul observed, we are all parts of an interdependent and complex body. Each has a role to play.

A small number of Christians will be called to the ordained ministry, a very important calling in the church. It is the ordained—from bishops to local pastors—who have the primary responsibility for seeing to it that the main purposes of the church discussed under "The Church as a Place of Responsibility" are carried out effectively. Their gifts and interests must be commensurate with what is required by those purposes. Obviously no one ordained person can possess or develop all those abilities equally. Wise church administrators will match up needs with abilities. But the unique gifts of the ordained—the articulation of the Word and the administration of the sacraments—are a crucial requisite for that calling.

The vast majority of Christians will find their calling in the church as laity. What kinds of disciplined attachment are available to them? We propose two basic poles of lay involvement, with perhaps the majority of lay people finding their calling somewhere between the two poles. The poles can be called the minimax and the maximin.

By minimax we mean a minimal commitment to one's calling in the church and a maximal commitment to worldly callings. For example, political figures may find the demands of their calling so great that they have little time left over for involvement in the church, particularly after they have given appropriate time to their spouse and family. Mothers with small children may be in similar circumstances. Those who are deeply absorbed in the activities of voluntary associations other than the church may have little time or energy for it.

Such commitment to worldly callings should not lead to guilt pangs on the part of laity. Nor should it lead to recriminations by the church on those laity. After all, the church exists to prepare and send people into the world. Rather, the church should affirm and support those laity as they work out their callings in marriage and family, work, and public life. One of the prime challenges of the church is precisely to encourage such ministries of the laity.

Nevertheless, along with a maximal commitment to worldly callings goes at least a minimal commitment to the church. That minimal level amounts to three things. First, it means regular participation in

the nourishing functions of the church—hearing the Word and receiving the sacraments, worship and study. Without such participation it is difficult to see how Christians can grow in faith, love, and
hope. Second, it means financial support for the church. Contributions should be proportionate to income. Third, it means involvement in at least one of the six functions of the church. With such a
variety of needs in the church's life, even minimal involvement
should include taking some responsibility for one of the following:
worship, study, administration, community, service, evangelism, or
ecumenical concern.

The other pole of lay calling in the church is the maximin. Laity
on this side of the ledger are called to maximal involvement in the
church. They are the ones with multiple commitments—serving on
church council, teaching Sunday school, representing the church at
various levels of the church's life, calling on prospective new members, visiting the sick, or serving on the social ministry committee.
Obviously, no one lay person can or should do all those things. Yet
it is amazing how many laity do make such extensive churchly commitments. Some of them are given consecrated or professional positions and roles within the church.

Such heavy absorption in the church's life generally means less
time and energy for worldly callings. Again, like the minimax types,
a reasonable commitment must be maintained in those worldly
places of responsibility.

Most laity will find themselves somewhere between those two
poles. Many may find that over time they may oscillate between the
poles. There are times in the life cycle—at retirement, for example—
when the possibilities for church involvement increase significantly.
But there is no simple formula for stipulating the proper level.

LOVE

The church, like all earthly institutions, is built on a network of
mutual relations and loyalties that are of greater or lesser stability.
Further, the church experiences its own share of sinful disruption of
those mutualities and loyalties, as anyone familiar with the church
can attest. At the same time the church should have resources of
reconciling love to heal its own wounds and to send it into service

to the world. The love of God in Christ for all sinners is the heart of its message, and such love should be reflected in the lives of those who make up the church.

The church should therefore be both a "school for Christian love" and a demonstration project of that love. Christians who take their calling within the life of the church seriously have many occasions to contribute their love. Christian love is expressed *in* the church, *through* the church, and *for* the church.

Love is expressed *in* the church. One of the most persuasive characteristics of the early church was the love shown among Christian brothers and sisters. So it continues today. Churches are places where pastoral care is expressed for members in need. When my wife's mother was hospitalized for many months, it was the network of care in our local parish that supported and consoled her. Ordained pastors are crucial in expressing this care, but lay people have just as important a role to play.

Love in its capacity for inclusiveness is expressed in the church. Worldly distinctions of status, class, race, and sex are transcended in authentic Christian community. All are loved as forgiven sinners for whom Jesus died.

Christian love as forgiveness and new beginning is also a mark of Christian community. As Christians greet each other with the peace of God before the Eucharist, they come to each other in repentance and forgiveness. They clear the way among one another before they approach the table of the Lord. This readiness to forgive should have repercussions in all of the church's life, enabling it to overcome the bitterness and alienation that plague our fallen lives.

The love of those called to church life is also expressed *through* the church, particularly in its evangelism and service. As God so loved the world that he sent his only begotten Son, so Christians so love the world that they bear the saving message of that Son to all the world. Such love is accompanied by service—social care and action. Service is both charity and the quest for justice.

The church, again like all worldly institutions, has tendencies toward self-centeredness. It is the love of its members that pulls it out of its introspection toward its mission in the world. Only as it moves out of itself can it become a fit instrument of the Spirit.

Finally, Christian love can be shown *for* the church. There are occasions which call for sacrificial love by Christians for their church. Ours is not a quid-pro-quo relation to the church. We are called to sacrifice for its mission in the world. Time, money, talents, and energy are our sacrifices to God and his work through the church.

HOPE

Just as faith and love are nurtured in the church by the Spirit and then double back to strengthen and extend the church, so hope manifests the same dynamic. We are brought to hope by the gospel as it is communicated by the church. But then the hope of ordinary saints serves to lighten the future of the church itself and of its relation to the world.

Christian hope gives present energy to Jesus' prayer that we might be one in him. We work in hope for the day when all Christians will be drawn together by the source of their oneness, Jesus Christ. Hope strives for more clarity in the marks of the church — its oneness, holiness, catholicity, and apostolicity. And it strains to make the church a foretaste of the things to come.

But Christian hope for the church is not only for the sake of the church, but also for the sake of the world. For it is in the church that we receive the clearest signals of God's intentions for the whole world. The mystical communion of Christians foreshadows the communion of the whole universe of being in the coming kingdom of God. Hope for the church is also hope for the world.

The whole of Christian life is a corollary of our justification by God's grace in Christ. The saving Word precedes everything else. Just as it is likely that Israel's experience of liberation in the exodus event came before her full interpretation of the world—its creation and moral order—so our reception of God's liberating grace in Christ precedes our construal of the world in faith, love, and hope. Following from that, the Spirit works in us and through us to bring forth the fruits of faith.

The gifts of the Spirit—faith, love, and hope—are the occasion for great joy. No one regrets having been given them. On the contrary, they enable us ordinary saints to celebrate all the other grand gifts of God's creation, as well as to bear the tragedies and faults of our broken lives. They bring a peace and joy that the world cannot give.

The final note we strike should be one of hope. To that end I quote Luther:

> This life is not righteous, but growth in righteousness; it is not health, but healing; not being, but becoming; not rest, but exercise; we are not yet what we shall be, but we are growing toward it; the process is not yet finished, but it is going on; this is not the end, but it is the road; all does not yet gleam in glory, but all is being purified.

BIBLIOGRAPHY

For a fuller picture of the fascinating Christian discipleship
of Dag Hammarskjöld:

Hammarskjöld, Dag. *Markings.* New York: Alfred A. Knopf, 1964.

For additional study in sociology of religion:

Berger, Peter. *The Precarious Vision.* Garden City, N.Y.: Doubleday & Co., 1961.
———. *The Sacred Canopy: Elements of a Sociological Theory of Religion.* New York: Doubleday & Co., 1969.

On the purposes of the church:

Hefner, Philip. "The Church." In *Christian Dogmatics,* edited by Carl E. Braaten and Robert W. Jenson, 2:179–247. Philadelphia: Fortress Press, 1984.

On the social mission of the church:

McDonagh, Edna. *The Church and Politics: From Theology to a Case History of Zimbabwe.* Notre Dame, Ind.: University of Notre Dame Press, 1980.
Niebuhr, H. Richard. "The Responsibility of the Church for Society." In *The Gospel, the Church, and the World,* edited by K. S. Latourette. New York: Harper & Brothers, 1946.

On ecumenical consensus:

Faith and Order Commission, World Council of Churches. *Baptism, Eucharist and Ministry.* Geneva; 1982.

On sociology of the church:

Gustafson, James M. *Treasure in Earthen Vessels: The Church as a Human Community.* New York: Harper & Row, 1961; reprinted, Chicago: University of Chicago Press, 1985.

Niebuhr, H. Richard. *The Social Sources of Denominationalism.* New York: Merid-
ian Books, 1957.

On basic images of the church:

Dulles, Avery. *Models of the Church.* Dublin: Gill & Macmillan, 1976; New
York: Doubleday & Co., 1978.
Minear, Paul. *Images of the Church in the New Testament.* Philadelphia: Westmin-
ster Press, 1970.

The concluding quote by Luther is used by Martin Marty in his newsletter,
Context 18, no. 10 (May 15, 1986): 4.

Index